I Am Abraham

ABRAHAM 'WOLE HAASTRUP

I Am Abraham

Copyright 2023 by Abraham Wole Haastrup

ISBN 978–0-6453800-8-8

All rights reserved. No part of this book may be produced, stored in a retrieval system, or transmitted in any form or by any means – electronic, mechanical, photocopy, recording, scanning, or any other – except for brief quotations in printed reviews, without the permission of the publisher.

Published in Melbourne, Australia by
Global Kingdom Influence (GKI)
Biblical Truth, Leadership, & Christian Advocacy,
Coburg North, Vic 3058, Australia.

Unless otherwise indicated, Scripture quotations are from The New King James Version of the Holy Bible, copyright 1982 – Thomas Nelson, Inc. used by permission.

OTHER BOOKS BY THE SAME AUTHOR

1. God Still Speaks Today
2. High Praise
3. Obedience - The Secret of Miracles
4. In Remembrance of Me
5. Your Last Hope
6. The Secret of Divine Favour
7. The Christian Worker
8. Ebenezer (God Can Do it Again)
9. The Almighty Formulae
10. Nations at Rage
11. The FIRST VOICE
12. Overcoming Giants
13. The Third Epistles (A Leadership Reminiscence)

 Dedication

To

YAHWEH,

The I AM THAT I AM

The God of Abraham, Isaac, and Jacob

(Exodus 3:12-15, Psalm 48:14)

FOREWORD

One of the greatest needs that exist today is the need for mentors who can serve as fathers in the faith to a new generation of emerging leaders. Fortunately, I became aware of this need very early in my ministry and it resulted in me seeking out people who would impact my life as they vicariously passed on the lessons they had learned from their unfolding lives. One of the ways this occurred was by reading autobiographies of influential leaders.

Which brings me to this autobiography – "I AM ABRAHAM" by Abraham Adewole Haastrup - author, teacher and kingdom influencer. In writing this book, Abraham expresses the desire that "readers will come to appreciate the voices and values that have helped shape my life and destiny."

Abraham's gifts of teaching and wisdom make this book more than a valuable autobiography. It presents emerging leaders and indeed any others with a resource that will provide a valuable list of life-shaping principles and values. It will also serve as a guide for developing an intimate relationship with the God who wonderfully shaped Abraham's life and destiny.

Abraham's dependence on God's word and the Holy Spirit

is most noticeable in his unfolding journey, and it is this practice that results in his growing ability to hear God's voice that is foundational in all he has done.

The book could be well used for both group and individual study with the suggestion that readers take time to record all the valuable lessons that are contained in Abraham's journey, even "lessons from the mistakes I have made."

I valued Abraham's wisdom in explaining how "God uses handicaps as raw materials for miracles" and that "for every mandate (or commission) God gives, He has His methods of getting it fulfilled", and "the two issues that continued to shape my life and destiny: God's voice and (learned) 'principles and practices.'"

Reading Abraham's autobiography has been an inspiring and educational experience for me and I affirm Abraham in his desire that "As you read, may you be inspired and also drawn closer to the same living God that created, preserved, saved and made a meaning out of a life that could have amounted to nothing."

I commend Abraham's autobiography as a valuable resource for all who are looking for a mentor to help them grow to their full potential in the calling that God has on their lives.

Rod Denton

Equipping The Next Generation, Adelaide, AUSTRALIA.
(www.roddentoning.com.au)

 # PREFACE

The question that may agitate some minds is: Why write an autobiography?

A Biography is a text written about someone else's life. The purpose of a biography is to unveil a man - his lifestyle, culture, the spiritual and intellectual forces that shaped his behavior and drove his life. It must be true because it is connected with reality. It must also be lively and creative because it is a form of literature that is lively and dynamic. It contains the facts of a man's life - birth, parentage, roots, calling, etc., but it must also contain the lessons that life teaches. It may raise issues located in the past, but it must also address the great subject of the present and the concerns of the future.[1]

An Autobiography, on the other hand, is the life story of the author – a written record of the author's life. There is nobody who can ever be able to tell our story like ourselves! In writing about personal experiences, one discovers himself.

I believe that through this book, *I am Abraham,* the readers will catch a glimpse of me – how God in His infinite mercies helped me to make a self-discovery. In particular, I believe readers will come to appreciate the voice and values that helped to shape my life and destiny. The purpose of this autobiography is, therefore, to share my story.

I believe that some lives will be affected for good by my story. To God be all the glory!

 **TABLE OF CONTENTS**

Other Books by the Same Author:	iv
Dedication	v
Foreword	vi
Preface	ix
Table of Contents	x
Introduction	viii
THE GOD OF ABRAHAM	1
1.1 THE ALMIGHTY	3
1.2 THE UNSTOPPABLE GOD!	7
1.3 A COVENANT-KEEPING GOD!	12
1.4 THE EVER-FAITHFUL GOD	15
1.5 THE ALPHA AND OMEGA	20
1.6 DON'T MESS UP WITH ABRAHAM!	23
I AM ABRAHAM	27
2.1 IN THE BEGINNING	29
2.2 REDEMPTIVE PURPOSE	45
2.3 SALVATION	54
2.4 THE CALL TO MINISTRY	58
ON A MISSION FOR JESUS	69
3.1 THE MANDATE	71
3.2 THE METHODS	85
3.3 THE MISTAKES	94

| 3.4 | THE MEDALS | 101 |
| 3.5 | WELCOME TO PATMOS | 112 |

THE VOICE AND VALUES OF DESTINY		118
4.1	THE VOICE OF DESTINY	120
4.2	THE VOICE TO ME AND FOR ME	124
4.3	LIFE-SHAPING VALUES AND PRINCIPLES	127
4.4	PUSHED INTO DESTINY	146
4.5	LIVING TESTIMONIES	157
4.6	ONCE, I WAS YOUNG	161

TO WHOM MUCH IS GIVEN		172
5.1	TO WHOM MUCH IS GIVEN	174
5.2	POSSESSING YOUR POSSESSION	184
5.3	LONGING FOR THE EVENING!	194
5.4	APPROACHING GOD'S PRESENCE	200
5.5	SPIRITUAL READING OF THE WORD	207

Afterword	223

Bible Study Outlines	228
Understanding God	230
Released Into Your Destiny	272
Behold, He Cometh!	294

Appendix:	319
Notes	324
Acknowledgments	326
Author's Full Profile	329

INTRODUCTION

One of the things that attracted my attention early in my Christian life, as God helped me to begin to personally study the Bible, is the story of the man ABRAHAM. His story (and that of his children, as well as Israel - the nation that grew out of them), is told in more than three quarters of the Holy Bible - that golden Book of books!

In the following pages is a personal account of a unique, God-given life that God has helped me to live. Born in Ilesha, South-West Nigeria on Friday, the 11th of January, 1952, I have tried to tell my own story from infancy to seventy years – the official retirement age in the Redeemed Christian Church of God (RCCG). The RCCG is a Pentecostal/Evangelical Church Body that started in Nigeria in 1952. I joined the church in August 1981, shortly after I gave my life to Jesus.

In this book, I have tried to capture how God used the story of ABRAHAM - the Biblical Patriarch of faith, to help me discover my own redemptive purpose and gifts, and in the ultimate, my personal destiny. Of great significance to me is the section of this book that enumerated the voice and values that combined to shape my life and destiny.

Also, included in this book are outlines of Bible Study materials inspired and taught by the help of the Holy Spirit. The Outlines are on three core topics:

- Understanding GOD
- Released Into Personal Destiny.
- Behold, He Cometh.

As you read, may you be inspired, and also be drawn closer to the same living God that created, preserved, saved, and made a meaning out of a life that could have amounted to NOTHING!

TO GOD BE ALL THE GLORY!

PART 1

THE GOD OF ABRAHAM

| 1.1 | THE ALMIGHTY |

| 1.2 | THE UNSTOPPABLE GOD! |

| 1.3 | A COVENANT-KEEPING GOD! |

| 1.4 | THE EVER-FAITHFUL GOD |

| 1.5 | THE ALPHA AND OMEGA |

| 1.6 | DON'T MESS UP WITH ABRAHAM! |

1.1

THE ALMIGHTY

The God of Abraham is the Almighty God. It is disheartening that some people still doubt the existence of God, or that He created and made them whatever they are. Psalm 14:1, says:

"The fool has said in his heart, "There is no God." They are corrupt, They have done abominable works, There is none who does good." (See also Psalm 53:1; Rom 1:18-20)

In Deuteronomy 8:12-18, God warned the Israelites:

"12 For when you have become full and prosperous and have built fine homes to live in, 13 and when your flocks and herds have become very large and your silver and gold have multiplied along with everything else, be careful! 14 Do not become proud at that time and forget the LORD your God, who rescued you from slavery in the land of Egypt. 15 Do not forget that he led you through the great and terrifying wilderness with its poisonous snakes and scorpions, where it was so hot and dry. He gave you water from the rock! 16 He fed you with manna in the wilderness, a food unknown to your ancestors. He did this to humble you and

test you for your own good. ¹⁷ He did all this so you would never say to yourself, 'I have achieved this wealth with my own strength and energy.' ¹⁸ Remember the LORD your God. He is the one who gives you power to be successful, in order to fulfill the covenant he confirmed to your ancestors with an oath."

It appears that the affluence in many of our western nations today has made us full, and we have already forgotten the One who gave us the power to make wealth! May God have mercy upon us all.

For our purpose here, it is important to emphasize and remind ourselves of some things regarding God:

In terms of His nature and character, God is Holy. He is also faithful, loving, and very merciful.

In terms of His power, God is the ALMIGHTY. He introduced Himself to Abraham in Gen 17:1,

"When Abram was ninety-nine years old, the Lord appeared to Abram and said to him, "I am Almighty God; walk before Me and be blameless."

The Bible also described God as the LORD Jehovah (the God of Heaven and Earth). He is the Creator of all. He is the great Redeemer, the great Restorer, etc. Not only is He the God of Abraham the Almighty, but He is also the Sovereign God.

God's Sovereignty means:

- God is superior and supreme. That is, He is greater than all, and He is above all (Isaiah 40:18, 25).

- God can do anything (Psalm 115:3). It should be noted, however, that God is not arbitrary - He works by principles!

- God can use anything, anywhere, and at any time to achieve His desires, His purposes, and His plans.

Also, by sovereignty, it means that God has the final or last say in all matters. This means when He says yes, no man can say no. When He opens, no one can close. When He has not said a matter is over, the chapter is not yet closed. When He says you will live, even when the enemy has put you in the grave, my Father can open the grave and bring you out! Perhaps as you are reading this, you or someone you know has a death sentence hanging over you, I decree in the mighty name of Jesus, you will not die, you will live, you will declare the glory of God!

God does not see as men see (1 Samuel 16:7; Matthew 6:4, 6). More than three times in the Book of Revelation, God called Himself the Alpha and Omega – the beginning and the ending, the first and the last (Revelations 1:8, 11, 18; 22:13).

I observe that the words that we speak and the songs we sing are composed of letters A-Z (or their equivalent in other languages). Also, to carry out all their evil activities, Satan and all his agents also use words! - (whether to afflict, to bring sickness, or to trouble people's destiny).

So, when Jesus says He is the Alpha and Omega, it means that before the enemy started their evil agenda, our God is far ahead of them, and their plan cannot succeed.

In Job 5:8-16 (NLT), the friends of Job advised him:

"If I were you, I would go to God and present my case to him. He does great things too marvellous to understand. He performs countless miracles. He gives rain for the earth and water for the fields. He gives prosperity to the poor and protects those who suffer. He frustrates the plans of schemers so the work of their hands will not succeed. He traps the wise in their own cleverness so their cunning schemes are thwarted. They find it is dark in the daytime, and they grope at noon as if it were night. He rescues the poor from the cutting words of the strong, and rescues them from the clutches of the powerful. And so at last the poor have hope, and the snapping jaws of the wicked are shut."

May this great God continue to be our God in Jesus' name!

1.2

THE UNSTOPPABLE GOD!

The God of Abraham is the Unstoppable God. The word *"unstoppable"* has been defined as something or someone incapable of being stopped. Other words for unstoppable are indomitable, insurmountable, unbeatable, unconquerable, invincible, etc.

The word *"unstoppable"* is a very important attribute of God. When we say God is holy, unchangeable, reliable, dependable, etc., it is easy to understand. However, when God is said to be unstoppable, many don't really understand that God is truly unstoppable!

Nothing can stop God! Rather than being stopped, God often uses the stopper as a stepping stone. I pray for you, dear reader, that all who had been trying to stop you from doing God's will shall become stepping stones to your promotion in Jesus' name. (If you believe this, please shout a loud *"Amen"* to it)!

In practical terms, to be stoppable means something or

someone could be hindered, blocked, locked in, locked out, locked up, or locked down. It also means that a person or thing could be prevented from making progress - whether upward, downward, forward, or even backward. It is understood that there are times when downward or backward movements could be progress in disguise. At such times, one needs to retire in order to refire!

There are at least three to four ways or levels at which something or someone could be stopped:

Firstly, someone could be prevented or stopped from starting, for example, a project or program.

Secondly, someone could be prevented from making progress – He or she may be stagnating or marking time at one point!

Thirdly, someone could be prevented from completing what has been started. In Ezra 4:4-6, we read of attempts made to stop Ezra and his team of builders. In the book of Nehemiah, the goal of Sanballat and Tobiah was to prevent Nehemiah from making progress or completing what God sent him to do. In both cases, the adversaries did all they could, but they failed. I pray again for you, dear reader, that everything the devil may try to stop you from making progress or finishing well will fail in Jesus' Name.

Fourth and lastly, someone could be prevented from enjoying what he or she has completed. In Isaiah 65:21-23, God promised the Israelites:

"They shall build houses and inhabit them; They shall plant vineyards and eat their fruit. They shall not build and another inhabit; They shall not plant and another eat; For as the days of a tree, so shall be the days of My people, And My elect shall long enjoy the work of their hands. They shall not labor in vain, Nor bring forth children for trouble; For they shall be the descendants of the blessed of the Lord, And their offspring with them."

May all these promises of our God become a reality in our lives in Jesus' name. When we therefore, talk about the Unstoppable God, we mean a God that nothing (no thing) could hinder from reaching His goals. Absolutely nothing, and no one – whether physical, spiritual, demonic, human, institutional, friends, lovers, or haters – nothing can stop our God! When you are connected with this Unstoppable God, especially when you carry His DNA in you, you too will become unstoppable.

Why can't God be stopped? There are several reasons:

* He cannot be stopped because of who He is - He is the Almighty, Sovereign.

* Also, God cannot be stopped because He is a Spirit.

 I AM ABRAHAM

Among the characteristics of spirits are that they are not visible to the physical eyes. In addition, walls cannot hinder them – they can enter a place without passing through doors! Hence, no walls or locked doors can hinder or prevent God from reaching you when your miracles are due.

* God cannot be stopped also, because He is God, and NOT a man.

There are several stories in the Bible – of individuals and nations – that prove beyond doubt that God is unstoppable. From the lives of Joseph, Mordecai, David, and Daniel, among others, we see an unstoppable God at work.

Even the stories of Israel as a nation shows it:

* Is it Israel's deliverance from Egypt one wants to talk about? To prevent it, there was nothing Pharaoh did not do! Yet, the Unstoppable God still brought out His people. (See Exod. 12:40-42)

* In Babylon, even when all hope was lost, God still did what He said He would do.

Psalm 126:1-3 declares:

"When the Lord brought back the captivity of Zion, We were like those who dream. Then our mouth was filled with laughter, And

our tongue with singing. Then they said among the nations, "The Lord has done great things for them." The Lord has done great things for us, And we are glad."

After Jesus' death on the cross, and He was buried, the Bible recorded (in Matthew 27:62-66, and Matthew 28:2-8), that there was nothing the killers did not do to try and stop Him from rising. But they failed because nothing can stop God. If there is anything the enemy has done or is doing to prevent you from fulfilling God's agenda for your life, today, may they begin to fail woefully in Jesus' name! Amen.

THE UNSTOPPABLE GOD of Abraham is still alive, and He can make you too unstoppable!

1.3

A COVENANT-KEEPING GOD!

The God of Abraham is a covenant-keeping God. He is a God who cannot lie. When He makes promises, He will surely keep them. Now, a covenant is a formal and serious agreement or promise. It is usually solemn, binding, and often sealed with blood.

God and Covenant

There were very few people in the Bible with whom God made or had a direct covenant. They include Abraham, Phineas, David (Genesis 17:1-8; Numbers 25:1-6, 7-13; Psalm 89:20-35); and Solomon (1 Kings 9:1-9). In each case, it was a "forever" or an "everlasting" covenant. God always kept His side – in as much as man does not default. Even when there is a default, God still gives room for repentance, restitution, restoration (or recovery), and a new beginning.

If, and when all His appeals are ignored, and man fails to heed His appeals, God will permanently stop the operation of the covenant and the flow of the blessings

associated with the covenant! At times, out of His extreme mercy, He may, however, retain the blessing for a remnant in the line of the original covenant partner. For example,

- Abraham - Isaac, Jacob, Joseph, and Levi.

- David - because of the sins of Solomon, only one out of twelve tribes was left to Rehoboam "for the sake of my servant David."

- In the case of Eli, God took away the entire priestly line from his father's line (1 Samuel 2:30-36).

In relation to God and His covenant, there is a law that should attract our attention: *the law of Precedence*. This law simply states that whatever God did before, He can, and He will do again! (provided the conditions are fulfilled, and His Sovereignty permits Him to do so). This means the way God acted or reacted to the issue of covenants, as well as those He was in covenant with, in Biblical times is the same way He would act and react today; even in our generation of Christianity, or church and denomination (Malachi 3:6, Hebrews 13:8).

If we keep the terms of the covenant intact, the blessings will continue to flow unhindered. If for anything we default, derail, or become presumptuous, then there are only two possibilities: total withdrawal of the blessings, or a leaving of a little blessing for a remnant faithful.

Hence, wisdom demands that we pay attention to the terms of the covenant, and be strict about adherence to the conditions. It also means that we should not spare deviants (Matthew 18:7-9). Passages like Genesis 39:7-9, 2 Kings 5:20-27, Acts 5:1-10, etc., make this law clearer.

In 1 Corinthians 10:6, 11-13, we read:

"6Now these things were our examples, to the intent we should not lust after evil things, as they also lusted...11 Now all these things happened unto them for ensamples: and they are written for our admonition, upon whom the ends of the world are come. 12 Wherefore let him that thinketh he standeth take heed lest he fall. 13 There hath no temptation taken you but such as is common to man: but God is faithful, who will not suffer you to be tempted above that ye are able; but will with the temptation also make a way to escape, that ye may be able to bear it."

All these tell us that anyone who does what each of these people (Joseph, Gehazi, Ananias and his wife, etc.) did, could expect to get the same reward or punishment they got. This is irrespective of who that person is, or where he or she came from, or even where he/she is located – be it Africa, Australia, UK, China, Japan, or America.

1.4

THE EVER-FAITHFUL GOD

The God of Abraham is an Ever-faithful God. An important attribute of this God of Abraham is that He does not joke with His words. In fact, He places a very high premium upon His word – both His spoken, written, and living Word. Anyone, anywhere, either past or present, who trivializes or belittles God's Word – by promoting himself or herself above it – will be looking for trouble, a big trouble!

No matter how long it appears to take, whatever God says will come to pass. Also, no matter how many people gang up, or bind themselves with an oath, and are determined to hinder what God says He would do, all their efforts will be futile. In fact, God may decide to use all they have put together as a stepping stone to accomplish His purpose (Lamentations 3:37, Psalm 33:8-12).

In Genesis 15, when it appeared to Abraham that God seemed to have forgotten His promise to give him a child, a conversation ensued between him and God. The interaction went on up to verse 12. Then God told

Abraham many things that would happen – even up to four hundred years to come. This is where the faithfulness of God comes in.

Across the Bible, and in different generations, the faithfulness of God – that thing in Him that makes Him to stand by His Word – was testified to (See Deuteronomy 7:9, 1 Kings 8:56, Nehemiah 1:5, 1 Corinthians 1:9, Revelations 19:11).

In Exodus 12:40-42 (NLT), we read:

"⁴⁰ The people of Israel had lived in Egypt for 430 years. ⁴¹ In fact, it was on the last day of the 430th year that all the LORD's forces left the land. ⁴² On this night the LORD kept his promise to bring his people out of the land of Egypt. So this night belongs to him, and it must be commemorated every year by all the Israelites, from generation to generation."

Has God specifically given you His Word, and it appears that the likelihood of the promise coming to pass is remote? Don't give up, don't lose faith. Remember Abraham. Romans 4:17-25 (NLT) says:

"¹⁷ That is what the Scriptures mean when God told him, "I have made you the father of many nations." This happened because Abraham believed in the God who brings the dead back to life and who creates new things out of nothing. ¹⁸ Even when there was no reason for hope, Abraham kept hoping—believing that he

would become the father of many nations. For God had said to him, "That's how many descendants you will have!" [19] *And Abraham's faith did not weaken, even though, at about 100 years of age, he figured his body was as good as dead—and so was Sarah's womb.* [20] *Abraham never wavered in believing God's promise. In fact, his faith grew stronger, and in this he brought glory to God.* [21] *He was fully convinced that God is able to do whatever he promises.* [22] *And because of Abraham's faith, God counted him as righteous.* [23] *And when God counted him as righteous, it wasn't just for Abraham's benefit. It was recorded* [24] *for our benefit, too, assuring us that God will also count us as righteous if we believe in him, the one who raised Jesus our Lord from the dead.* [25] *He was handed over to die because of our sins, and he was raised to life to make us right with God."*

God will still do what He says (Numbers 23:19, Isaiah 40:8). Also, in Isaiah 65:22 (NLT), we read:

"Unlike the past, invaders will not take their houses and confiscate their vineyards. For my people will live as long as trees, and my chosen ones will have time to enjoy their hard-won gains."

When something is set apart or dedicated to God, one must be careful not to toy with such a thing or such a person. We see all across the Bible how God jealously watched over that which was dedicated to Him, or what He took as His own:

- King Abimelech vs. Abraham (Gen 26:1-18).

- Lot vs. Abraham (Gen 13:1-18).

- Laban vs. Jacob (Gen 31:22-55).

- Joseph vs. his brothers (Gen 45:1-8).

- Joseph vs. Mrs. Potiphar (Gen 39:7-23).

- Haman vs. the Jews (Esther 7:1-10; 8:1-17).

Psalm 89:22-24 further reiterates this. One can go on and on. The case of Joseph was particularly interesting. In Genesis 45:1-8 (NLT), we read:

"Joseph could stand it no longer. There were many people in the room, and he said to his attendants, "Out, all of you!" So he was alone with his brothers when he told them who he was. ² Then he broke down and wept. He wept so loudly the Egyptians could hear him, and word of it quickly carried to Pharaoh's palace. ³"I am Joseph!" he said to his brothers. "Is my father still alive?" But his brothers were speechless! They were stunned to realize that Joseph was standing there in front of them. ⁴ "Please, come closer," he said to them. So they came closer. And he said again, "I am Joseph, your brother, whom you sold into slavery in Egypt. ⁵ But don't be upset, and don't be angry with yourselves for selling me to this place. It was God who sent me here ahead of you to preserve your lives. ⁶ This famine that has ravaged the land for two years will last five more years, and there will be neither

plowing nor harvesting. ⁷ God has sent me ahead of you to keep you and your families alive and to preserve many survivors. ⁸ So it was God who sent me here, not you! And he is the one who made me an adviser to Pharaoh—the manager of his entire palace and the governor of all Egypt."

While the hatred and envy of Joseph's brothers grew, and they decided to get rid of him, God had an entirely different plan. Somehow, He did not let them kill Joseph. Eventually, this Almighty God directed the steps of the Midianite traders to be near, and He made Joseph's brothers bring him out of the cistern, and sell him to them. At the end of the day, it became clear that while Joseph's brothers sold him to get rid of him and his dreams, God indeed sent him ahead to preserve posterity. Are you in a place because men *"sold"* you there in order to get rid of you? Rejoice! Begin to see the big picture – God sent you, and it is to make you great, and then use you to preserve posterity.

1.5

THE ALPHA AND OMEGA

⁸ "I am the Alpha and the Omega, the Beginning and the End," says the Lord, "who is and who was and who is to come, the Almighty."... 11 saying, "I am the Alpha and the Omega, the First and the Last," and, "What you see, write in a book and send it to the seven churches which are in Asia: to Ephesus, to Smyrna, to Pergamos, to Thyatira, to Sardis, to Philadelphia, and to Laodicea."... ¹⁸ I am He who lives, and was dead, and behold, I am alive forevermore. Amen. And I have the keys of Hades and of Death. (Revelations 1:8, 11, 18)

The God of Abraham is also the Alpha and Omega. He is the Beginning and the Ending. He is the First and the Last. One of the ways He manifested this special attribute is that he called the things that be not as though they were. Another way in which He shows it, is that He uses what human beings call "handicaps" as raw materials for greatness! For instance, this great God saw that Abraham had a particularly serious need. The man Abraham and his wife Sarah had been barren for years. In Romans 4:17-21 (NLT), we see a clearer picture of how remote and far beyond human calculation the situation of Abraham and his wife was:

"¹⁷That is what the Scriptures mean when God told him, "I have made you the father of many nations. "This happened because Abraham believed in the God who brings the dead back to life and who creates new things out of nothing. ¹⁸ Even when there was no reason for hope, Abraham kept hoping—believing that he would become the father of many nations. For God had said to him, "That's how many descendants you will have!" ¹⁹ And Abraham's faith did not weaken, even though, at about 100 years of age, he figured his body was as good as dead—and so was Sarah's womb. ²⁰ Abraham never wavered in believing God's promise. In fact, his faith grew stronger, and in this he brought glory to God. ²¹ He was fully convinced that God is able to do whatever he promises."

Thank God that Abraham's faith and trust in God were unshakeable. Verse 18 in the above Scriptures says, *"Even when there was no reason for hope, Abraham kept hoping—believing that he would become the father of many nations. For God had said to him, "That's how many descendants you will have!"*

Are human beings looking at you and all they see are your "handicaps"? Don't see what they see! Rather, see God – the God who uses handicaps as raw materials for miracles. See His Almightiness. See His sovereignty. See God's

faithfulness. See His antecedents. See what He did before especially on the pages of the Holy Bible. Know that He is the unchangeable God, the One who can do what He did before. See what God sees; see yourself as a potential miracle – a work-in-progress in the Hands of the Master Sculptor! At different times in my life, I have seen the awesome move of God, and the fact that He can repeat miracles.

1.6

Don't Mess Up With Abraham!

In His sovereignty, God – the Creator of Heaven and the Earth – peeped down from Heaven, and located the family of a man called Terah. Terah, then was living in a town called Ur in the Mesopotamia Region of today's Middle East. The man Terah had three sons – Abram, Nahor, and Haran. God's spotlight was beamed on Abram. God made several promises to Abram. Attached to the seven promises are three things that God required Abram to do.

In Genesis 12:1-5 (NLT), we read:

"The LORD had said to Abram, "Leave your native country, your relatives, and your father's family, and go to the land that I will show you. ² I will make you into a great nation. I will bless you and make you famous, and you will be a blessing to others. ³ I will bless those who bless you and curse those who treat you with contempt. All the families on earth will be blessed through you." ⁴ So Abram departed as the LORD had instructed, and Lot went with him. Abram was seventy-five years old when he left Haran. ⁵

 I AM ABRAHAM

He took his wife, Sarai, his nephew Lot, and all his wealth—his livestock and all the people he had taken into his household at Haran—and headed for the land of Canaan. When they arrived in Canaan,"

The promises were later reiterated and sealed with a covenant agreement between God and Abram. In Genesis 17:1-14 (NLT), we read:

"When Abram was ninety-nine years old, the LORD appeared to him and said, "I am El-Shaddai—'God Almighty.' Serve me faithfully and live a blameless life. ² I will make a covenant with you, by which I will guarantee to give you countless descendants." ³ At this, Abram fell face down on the ground. Then God said to him, ⁴ "This is my covenant with you: I will make you the father of a multitude of nations! ⁵ What's more, I am changing your name. It will no longer be Abram. Instead, you will be called Abraham. for you will be the father of many nations. ⁶ I will make you extremely fruitful. Your descendants will become many nations, and kings will be among them! ⁷ "I will confirm my covenant with you and your descendants after you, from generation to generation. This is the everlasting covenant: I will always be your God and the God of your descendants after you. ⁸ And I will give the entire land of Canaan, where you now live as a foreigner, to you and your descendants. It will be their possession forever, and I will be their God." ⁹ Then God said to Abraham, "Your responsibility is to obey the terms of the covenant. You and all your descendants

have this continual responsibility. ¹⁰ This is the covenant that you and your descendants must keep: Each male among you must be circumcised. ¹¹ You must cut off the flesh of your foreskin as a sign of the covenant between me and you. ¹² From generation to generation, every male child must be circumcised on the eighth day after his birth. This applies not only to members of your family but also to the servants born in your household and the foreign-born servants whom you have purchased. ¹³ All must be circumcised. Your bodies will bear the mark of my everlasting covenant. ¹⁴ Any male who fails to be circumcised will be cut off from the covenant family for breaking the covenant."

Becoming a man of destiny was not an easy task for Abram. Years went by, and a nation grew from Abraham. That nation, Israel, took its name from Jacob – Abraham's grandson, who God later named Israel.

From our opening text, it is clear that as far as God is concerned, when we talk about the nations of the world, there are only two major classifications: Israel, on the one hand, and, on the other hand, all other nations combined! In His divine arrangement, the Almighty God has some expectations from all the nations towards Israel. In Isaiah 14:2, we read:

"² The nations of the world will help the people of Israel to return, and those who come to live in the LORD's land will serve them. Those who captured Israel will themselves be captured, and Israel will rule over its enemies."

Here, Israel is described as "the Lord's land". All the other nations are expected:

1. to help the people of Israel to return, and,

2. to come and live in the LORD's land and serve them (the Israelites). The 'return' here, has two dimensions – physical and spiritual. Physically – in 1948, Israel returned to the land. However, spiritually, they are yet to return to the LORD of the land. In this realm, all Nations owe Israel prayers for this to happen.

In addition,

3. the nations who attempt to capture Israel will themselves be captured, and,

4. Israel will rule over its enemies!

Thus, it behooves all the other nations to have a positive attitude towards Israel. They ought to treat the Lord's land with caution. Any nation that chooses to contend with or fight Israel will have God to contend with.

Hence, don't mess up with Abraham! Also, don't mess up with the seed of Abraham.

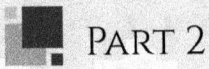

PART 2

I Am Abraham

2.1	IN THE BEGINNING
2.2	REDEMPTIVE PURPOSE
2.3	SALVATION
2.4	THE CALL TO MINISTRY

2.1

IN THE BEGINNING

⁴ The LORD gave me this message: ⁵ "I knew you before I formed you in your mother's womb. Before you were born I set you apart and appointed you as my prophet to the nations." (Jeremiah 1:4-5 NLT)

Many forces have the power or potential to influence, shape, and even determine what a person turns out to be in life. These include knowledge and ignorance. The others are the environment, the divine hand of God, the enemy's agenda, etc. Let us begin with knowledge. While knowledge is power, ignorance can be very dangerous (John 8:32, 36, Hosea 4:6).

What a person knows or refuses to know can form or deform him or her.

Environment

The environment in which a child grows – beginning right from the womb – goes a long way to determine what a child becomes in life. The struggles, rivalry, etc. between Jacob and Esau dated back to the womb! (Genesis 25:2023). It continued at birth (Genesis 25:26), and even as they grew up. Not too long ago, I met a woman (in her thirties). She said she started drinking and taking drugs with her mum from the age of three. Other environmental factors are religion, choices, habits, associations, and associates - peers, marriage partner, etc (Psalm 1:1-3; 1 Corinthians 15:33).

The Hand of God

The divine hand of God is another very important determinant in how a child turns out in life; when in particular, the one concerned could be described as a 'Child of Destiny' (a CoD). In this case, God uses all and whatever the enemy tries to do as tools to get such a CoD to the ultimate place and level He (the Almighty God) has in mind. Unless the so-called CoD refuses to cooperate with God, God would never abandon him or her. The stories of Abraham, Jacob, Joseph, Moses, David, Samson, Esther, Peter, Saul of Tarsus, etc. clearly illustrate this point (Please see Jeremiah 1:4-5; 29:11, Romans 9:15-16, Psalm 89:1; 22-24).

The Enemy Factor

Man has enemies; the number one being Satan (1 Peter 5:7-9). Others include powers of darkness, and the man himself – probably out of ignorance! The primary aim of the enemies is to waste lives and destinies – and they can do anything or use anything or anyone! (As seen in John 10:10, Ephesians 6:10-12). It is a person who cooperates with God through voluntary and submissive obedience (as against compelled, coerced, and necessitated obedience), that He works out His Master Plan for.

I want to specially thank God that His Word has overruled and outweighed a combination of possible factors or forces that could have worked together to derail my destiny. I can safely say that it is of the Lord's mercies that I have not been consumed (Lamentations 3:22-23). To Him be all the glory forever, in Jesus' name.

As earlier quoted, Jeremiah 1:4 (NLT) says:

"The lord gave me this message: "I knew you before I formed you in your mother's womb. Before you were born I set you apart and appointed you as my prophet to the nations."

As the divine hand of God was at work – even before this great Prophet was conceived, so I believe it is with me too. It is because YAHWEH – God, The I AM that I am, The God of Abraham, Isaac, and Jacob – knew me before I was formed in the womb, that is why He also supervised my conception, carrying, and eventual safe delivery on that Friday, 11th January 1952. This great God did not allow me to be malformed, deformed, miscarried, or be stillborn!

In addition to all these, God also did something extraordinary. It was my very mother - Florence Tinuola Abebi – who told me the story:

Before conceiving me, she already had four children - three boys and one girl. About three years plus seven months after raising my immediate senior brother (Adedeji), she discovered that she was pregnant. At the early part of her pregnancy, she was not feeling comfortable. Being already a true believer in Jesus (of the stock of The Apostolic Church), she went for a weekly prayer meeting, and a Seer (one of the elderly prophets in the Apostolic Church, Oke-Ooye, Ilesha, South-West, Nigeria), prayed for her, and told her in confidence that she was carrying a twin - a boy and girl! Rather than being excited, Mama broke down in tears. "Why?" one may ask. At that time, she was the second wife to David Adebiyi - an Ijesha prince and socialite who had grown in his penchant for acquiring women. He already had additional four wives and not less than four concubines! It had, therefore, been by the special grace of God, and the assistance of her mother (Deborah Adeola Otunla), that Florence (my mother), had been fending for herself and raising her children.

On returning home after departing from the Seer, she went into prayers (with fasting). She had just one request - that God would turn the two in her womb to a big one, preferably a boy. The time to deliver came. Lo and behold, it was a boy! This probably was why she felt that the only Biblical name she could give to the boy was ABRAHAM - "Apere Igbagbo" - (meaning 'an Evidence, a sign, or example of faith'). All these happened a little over Seventy years ago.

My mother was a great woman of faith. Though a second wife in a highly polygamous and somewhat idolatrous environment, her faith kept her strong and gave her a great edge. She never allowed anything or anyone to come in between her and her God. Eventually, God used her tremendously to bring the light of the Gospel into the home. God used her for the conversion of all other wives. They all were baptized and received new Biblical names. In fact, it was these names that all of us grew up to know all our other 'mothers' with.

My mother lived as a totally true Christian till she went to be with the Lord on the 14th of June 2002, at the ripe age of 92. It was a glorious departure. Even in death, God brought many souls to His Kingdom. A few weeks after all the burial ceremonies, I travelled back home (Ilesha) to see my dad. He thanked me and my brothers for giving our mother a glorious burial. Then he said he would love to go and be buried exactly the way we did for his wife - our mother. On that day, God gave me an unusual boldness to be frank with him. I told him that was not likely to happen.

I told him that my mother did not die, she only slept in the Lord, and that one day very soon, I would see her in heaven. I then told my dad that if he wanted to end as my mother did, and also be buried like her, he must surrender his life to Jesus, and be truly born again. To the glory of God, on that wonderful day, for the first time, my dad knelt and gave his life to Jesus. He passed away not too long thereafter.

Childhood Truancy

In growing up, I was not shielded from all that any boy growing up in my type of environment experienced – childhood rascality, stubbornness, and even truancy. My dad was a village chief who lived in the city. He only paid occasional visits to his base and spent most of his life in the town of Ilesha. On many occasions when he asked me and my other stepbrothers to follow him to the village, by the second or third day, I would abscond from the village and trek back to the town (Ilesha). Till today, how I, a boy aged between 14-15 years would trek those twelve miles (from the village to Ilesha) with all the dangers (both physical and spiritual), is still a mystery to me! Again, it was by the mercies of God that I was not consumed! (Lamentations 3:22-23).

The years 1963-1966 were very memorable in my life. It was a period when I, more or less, became "motherless!"

Early in 1963, my mother had to leave her base in Ilesha for the northern part of Nigeria, precisely Kano. It was part of the sacrifice a mother had to make in order to "hide away" in the far north where she could do any job, no matter how menial, to generate funds to pay for her children's education, especially that of the two senior ones. So, I more or less became *"motherless."*

Whenever this chapter of my life comes to my mind, I remember a story in Genesis 43. Joseph had been sold to slavery by his ten envious and hateful senior brothers. At the same time, Benjamin – a motherless child, the son of joseph's mother (Rachel), had been left with those same ten brothers. During those twenty-two years that Joseph had been away from home, he would have imagined or thought of what Benjamin may have been going through. Was he being treated in the same manner they did to him? Was Benjamin sick, being bullied, beaten, harassed, or was he even still alive? While others had the warm embrace and succor of their mothers, none could defend Benjamin!

When eventually the global famine that also hit Caanan brought Jacob's ten sons to Egypt, and they began to tell Joseph who they were and where they came from, Joseph was more interested in knowing about the only one that mattered to him in heaven and the earth – Benjamin, the other son of Joseph's mother. Thus, when he heard that the boy was still alive, he made bringing Benjamin a necessary and sufficient condition for them if they would ever see his face again. Eventually, Joseph's brothers returned to buy more corn. This time, they brought Benjamin with them. On that day, when Joseph set his eyes on Benjamin – the son of his mother, the Bible said in Gen 43:29-31 (NLT):

"29 Then Joseph looked at his brother Benjamin, the son of his own mother. "Is this your youngest brother, the one you told me about?" Joseph asked. "May God be gracious to you, my son." 30 Then Joseph hurried from the room because he was overcome with emotion for his brother. He went into his private room, where he broke down and wept. 31 After washing his face, he came back out, keeping himself under control. Then he ordered, "Bring out the food!"

Now, back to my own story. During the period 1963-1966, no one, in particular, was available that I could relate to as a mother. I oscillated living with my father, an uncle, an Apostolic Church Pastor/Evangelist, and later ended up at my grandmother's place! Ordinarily, the trauma of such a period was enough to turn a young boy like me into a vagabond. Again, I thank the Almighty God for His mercy.

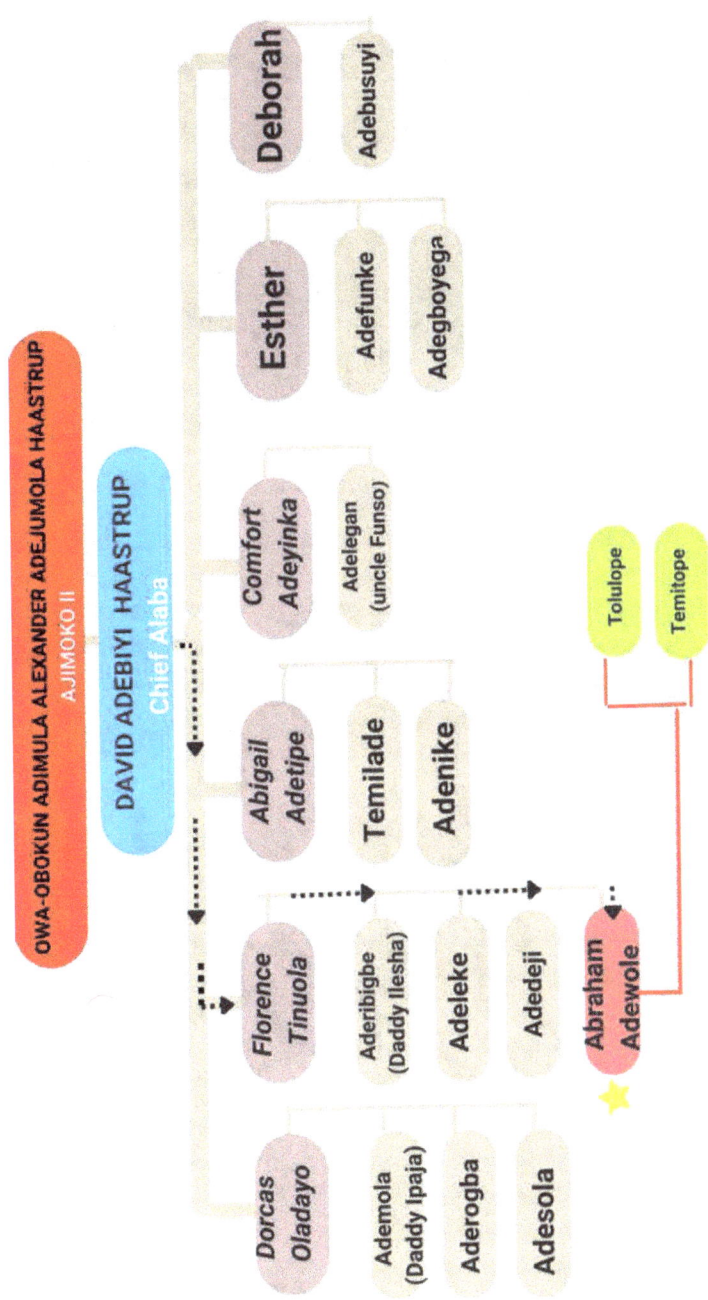

Abraham at Primary school (1963)

Abraham at secondary school (1970)

Abraham at secondary school (1972)

Abraham with a school mate @ Ibadan Polytechnic(1977)

Abraham on Matriculation Day (1977)

Abraham and Elder brother on Graduation Day (1980)

Abraham during National Youth service (1980)

Abraham with Ijesha Students' Association of University of Ibadan (1979)

Abraham with parent and siblings

Mama @90 with other wives

Mama @90 with friends

Abraham with his elder brothers

2.2

REDEMPTIVE PURPOSE

Further to His assertion in Jeremiah 1:4-5 (earlier quoted), God also through the man Jeremiah said in Jeremiah 29:11-14 (NLT):

"11 For I know the plans I have for you," says the LORD. "They are plans for good and not for disaster, to give you a future and a hope. 12 In those days when you pray, I will listen. 13 If you look for me wholeheartedly, you will find me. 14 I will be found by you," says the LORD. "I will end your captivity and restore your fortunes. I will gather you out of the nations where I sent you and will bring you home again to your own land."

One of the earliest things that God did as He started establishing me in the faith was to draw my attention to some Biblical personalities. One of them was the man - Abraham. Not too long after, I began to see my life in the light of this great patriarch of faith. Almost every aspect of his life has something for me to learn from. Particularly, how God, in His Sovereignty, sought Abraham out, called him, and made him a man of destiny still marvels me. Also, Abraham's faith in God, as well as what God did to reward

 I AM ABRAHAM

Abraham's faith piqued my interest. (Genesis 22:12-18, Romans 4:13; 17-21).

Talking about destiny, God made us all for a purpose. There is a great destiny to fulfill. Many a time, we are ignorant of the divine agenda, and we may even be working against it! The man Saul of Tarsus (who later became Apostle Paul), was all the while attacking and persecuting the very faith he was born to propagate (Galatians 1:15-24). As God did to Paul, He has done for many of us too. We thank God for His mercies that located us before we could destroy ourselves! Glory be to God!

ABRAHAM, the man to whom the Bible devoted threequarters of its pages, was a man of destiny. Coming from an idol-worshipping family did not stop God from focusing His love and attention on him. In Genesis 12:1-5 (NLT), we read:

"¹The lord had said to Abram, "Leave your native country, your relatives, and your father's family, and go to the land that I will show you. ²I will make you into a great nation. I will bless you and make you famous, and you will be a blessing to others. ³I will bless those who bless you and curse those who treat you with contempt. All the families on earth will be blessed through you." ⁴So Abram departed as the lord had instructed, and Lot went with him. Abram was seventy-five years old when he left Haran. ⁵He took his wife, Sarai, his nephew Lot, and all his wealth—his

livestock and all the people he had taken into his household at Haran — and headed for the land of Canaan. When they arrived in Canaan,"

God – who called Abraham and also honored His Word to make him a monumental person and a point of reference – is still very much alive. He is ever faithful. Several years ago, it dawned on me that God has a purpose for my life and that I am not an accident of nature. I just do not occur!

I believe this is also true for every person on this earth. The moment we are born again, (that is, we become a new creation), we must begin to crave the understanding of our purpose for living here on earth (2 Corinthians 5:17, Philippians 3:12).

To discover purpose, the following pointers will help:

- **Potentials** - Your in-built abilities, talents, and God-given gifts. The knowledge or skills you acquire in life should be to shape and sharpen your potential.

- **Passion** - The things you exceptionally have flare or zeal for, or do quite often with ease. Learn to build your vocation or career on such things.

- **Prayer** - After you have identified your potential (s), and the things you are passionate about, you need to pray for divine guidance and direction, so that the world and the enemy will not hijack your purpose in life!

As I look back, the reasons why I am in RCCG (and why God had kept me and lifted me this far) have become very clear. Among others, it is to speak, and bear witness to the Truth - that Truth that is worth dying for!

(Jeremiah 1:4-5, John 18:37, Psalm 101:1-10, Esther 4:13-14).

Abraham and Jane at Ikeja Marriage Registry (Jan 1986)

Abraham & Jane at RCCG Hdqs, Ebute-Metta, on our Wedding Day (1st Feb 1986).

Abraham & Jane with Daddy & Mummy Adeboye at RCCG Hdqs, Ebute-Metta, on our Wedding Day (1st Feb 1986).

Abraham & Jane with Senior Pastors at RCCG Hdqs, EbuteMetta, on our Wedding Day (1st Feb 1986).

Abraham & Jane at RCCG Hdqs, Ebute-Metta, a fortnight after wedding.

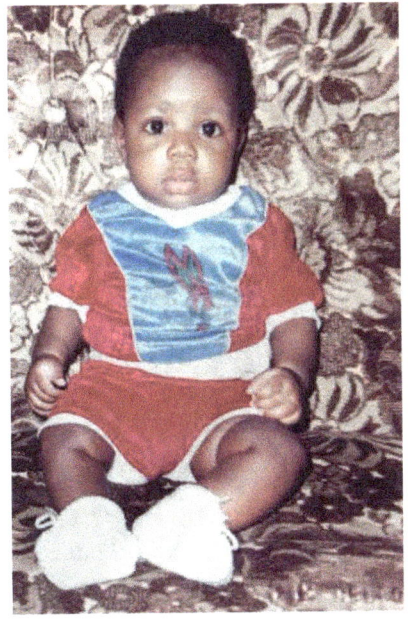

Baby Tolu - on a Sunday at RCCG Hdqs, Ebute-Metta, (June 1987).

Jane with Baby Tolulope at RCCG Hdqs, Ebute-Metta, on his Dedication (May 1987).

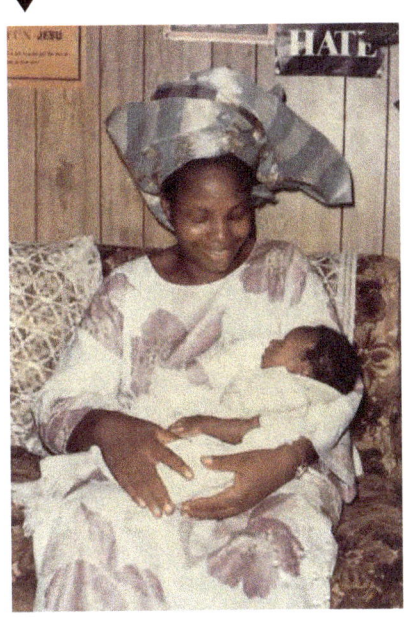

Tolu & Tope with their Aunty on excursion to International Airport Lagos (1992)

Abraham and Jane with Tolu and Tope (Ketu, Lagos, 1996

Abraham and family @ Oshogbo (1998)

Abraham & Jane at home in Oshogbo (1998)

Abraham & Jane at home in Oshogbo (1998)

Abraham & Jane at a function in Akure, Ondo State (2007).

2.3

SALVATION

"¹⁷This means that anyone who belongs to Christ has become a new person. The old life is gone; a new life has begun! ¹⁸ And all of this is a gift from God, who brought us back to himself through Christ. And God has given us this task of reconciling people to him. ¹⁹ For God was in Christ, reconciling the world to himself, no longer counting people's sins against them. And he gave us this wonderful message of reconciliation. ²⁰ So we are Christ's ambassadors; God is making his appeal through us. We speak for Christ when we plead, "Come back to God!" ²¹ For God made Christ, who never sinned, to be the offering for our sin, so that we could be made right with God through Christ," (2 Corinthians 5:17-21 NLT)

It is genuine salvation (or conversion) that opens a person to the discovery of God's redemptive purpose. The fulfillment, however, depends on a person's cooperation with God as shown in their uncompromising obedience (1 Samuel 15:22-23, Judges 16:1-25).

My Salvation Story

On Wednesday, 8th July 1981, in Owo (South-west Nigeria), at the Corpers' Fellowship, just two days to the end of my National Service year in Ondo State, I accepted Jesus into my life. The decision was the climax of a series of events, and health challenges, especially insomnia.

In my days as a student at the University of Ibadan, I was on different dosages of Valium to overcome insomnia; all to no avail. This had a lot of tolls on my studies and concentration. It grew to a worrisome level when one day, in my second year, during a semester examination, I entered the exam hall only to wake up in the University Health Centre. They said I had lost consciousness while writing one of the papers. I think they said the first words I uttered when I regained consciousness had to do with the particular question I was answering before I passed out. Again, by the mercy of God, I re-wrote the paper, passed, and still graduated with my set in July 1980.

Abraham and Family @ Tolu's Graduation in Newcastle, UK (2015)

Tope with Daddy Abraham (2017).

Tolu with Mummy Jane (2015)

Abraham & Jane at home in Melbourne - as part of preparations towards "W@70" (Dec 2021).

2.4

THE CALL TO MINISTRY

On September the 25th 1989, I left Lagos, Nigeria for the United Kingdom, having been selected for a British Government Technical Assistance by my employers - the Lagos State Government. It was a Post-Graduate Diploma Program in Development Finance at the University of Birmingham (West Midlands). With the Lord's help, I did very well in the program. At the end of the second semester, my performance had attracted the attention of my Department. I was, therefore, asked to come for a discussion.

A few days later, I got a letter from the University that my Post-Graduate Diploma Program had been upgraded to a Masters! It was nothing but a divine intervention. This was because I had been actively involved in Christian ministry with our Church - the RCCG (which just began her first branch ever, in London). This necessitated my traveling to London every weekend. Meanwhile, I had also started hosting a mid-week Christian Fellowship in my hostel (Edgbaston main campus), of the University, while also being an active member of the main University Christian Students' Fellowship.

The Call into Ministry and Missions

That God is real, and that He speaks are no more controvertible (Romans 1:18-21, Acts 10:1-7; 9-20). Perhaps what many people may have challenges with, is how to hear, discern the very voice of God, and also obey Him. In two earlier books ("God Still Speaks Today", Almond Books, Lagos, 1993; and "The First Voice", Sunrise Foundation International, Melbourne, 2017), all these have been extensively discussed.

I thank God that, somehow, He has given me the rare privilege of hearing and discerning His voice. In several ways, I get convinced that what I perceived God is saying to me is from Him. This conviction had come in different and diverse ways. On some occasions, God's voice had come through His Word - the Holy Bible. As I studied and meditated on God's Word, I had heard Him speak to my heart through a word, a phrase, a verse, and even through a Bible personality or character. There were occasions too when the Lord painted a scene before me. On other occasions, an experience described in the Scriptures was what He used to draw my attention to what He was trying to say to me. There were particular days when what I have come to group together as "Matters Arising" (see Appendices at the end of this book for more on Spiritual Reading of the Scriptures), would be what God used to instruct me. Such instructions could be an assurance, a direction to follow, a warning to heed, or a personality or place to avoid.

In many cases, God's Holy Spirit had dropped a verse of the Scriptures or an idea in my heart that was far beyond my mind or imagination. In the past too, God had used a great peace of mind (or the loss of it), on a matter, to let me know if I was on the right track or not. For example, in addition to speaking clearly about my going into full-time ministry, God also took the interest and enthusiasm for the work I was doing then, away. In the period before that, things were different. Even though it was a career job in the civil service, every day I woke up, I looked forward to a great working day. I was so committed that God began to drop ideas that I wrote down as proposals and submitted to higher authorities. They did not begin to implement a particular one until four years after I had left the service. To the God of all wisdom and knowledge be all the glory in Jesus' Name!

Another thing that God had used was a blockage or a disappointment, even when all evidence seems to say everything is perfect! In all things, the Word of God – the Holy Bible – remains the final arbiter on every matter. I will continue to be thankful to God for the sanctifying power of His Word, and how it has helped me to discern the mind of God. (John 17:17, Romans 12:1-2, 1Corinthians 2:9-11).

Given some levels of success and favors I received in my studies at the University of Birmingham, in April 1990, I decided to pursue a Ph.D. Program in Development Economics. So, I applied to some universities, and God opened the door for admission. Three universities - Cambridge, Glasgow, and my own, Birmingham, gave me admission into an M. Phil Program that would lead to a Ph.D. Then came May of the same year, and I started having some unsettling of mind - an indication that I might have taken some wrong steps. Initially, I did not pay serious attention to it. I rationalized it as one of those occasional issues that came and would soon fizzle away. This time, however, the matter persisted, and whenever I went to the university library to research materials or collect data, I could not concentrate.

Eventually, it became very clear that God was calling me into Missions. As I started looking for materials and information on Missions, I heard about The US Centre for International Missions (in Pasedena, California), and got in touch with them. I wrote Fuller Seminary School of World Missions. One particular Book - "Perspectives On World Christian Movements" - (compiled by Ralph Winter and Steve Hawthorne), was very, very helpful to me. Then, I got a book titled "OPERATION WORLD – it was 'a Definitive Daily Prayer Guide for Every Nation' it was compiled by Patrick Johnstone. In addition to all these, I began to take deeper interest in Mission policies, initiatives, and activities of the RCCG. By God's grace, in the last 30 years, I have served in many Mission outposts of RCCG. As part of the Reforms of 2006-2010, the Central Missions Board (CMB), was created. I have also written several papers advising our church on Missions:

(i) "Understanding Missions - An appraisal of RCCG Foreign Mission Activities"

(ii) "Reaching and Discipling The Natives - The Challenges of Missions"

To the glory of God and Him alone, in the last 3-4 years, I have been the Chairman of RCCG World Advisory Council (WAC).

In the Australia/Pacific Continent of RCCG (our current place of service), we recently introduced an Annual Evangelism and Missions Weekend - to pray for and sensitize our members on the centrality of Evangelism and Missions to the Church. Of course, in the Parish where I worship in Melbourne (RCCG Kings Court), every 3rd Sunday is our "Evangelism and Missions Sunday".

Abraham with LASG senior Officers on a Manpower Training Programme (UNILAG 1987).

Abraham with LASG senior Officers on a Manpower Training Programme (ASCON 1988).

Abraham and Jane being Prayed for by Leaders and Brethren LASG Christian Fellowship Alausa-Ikeja (at his send forth, March 1992).

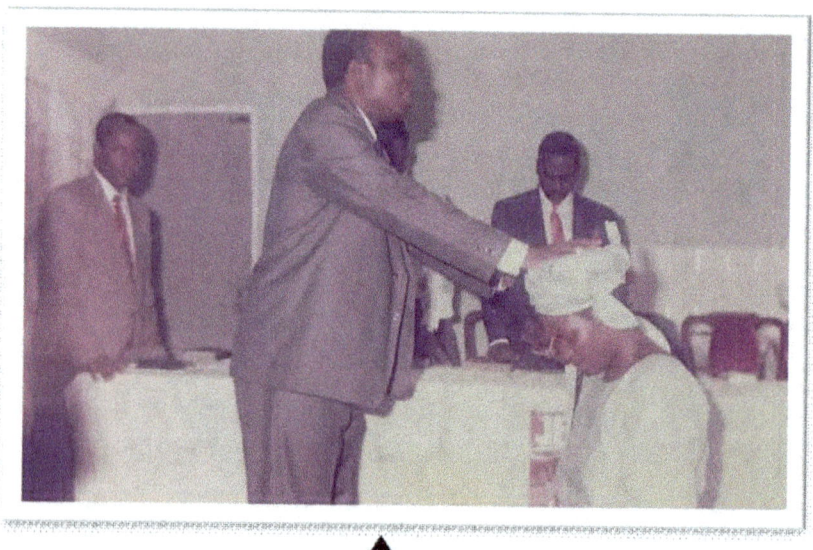

Abraham & Jane being Prayed for by Rev J.I. Akindele (LASG Christian Fellowship Alausa Ikeja, at his send forth, March 1992).

THE CALL TO MINISTRY

Abraham and Jane - Group photograph with Leaders and Brethren LASG Christian Fellowship Alausa-Ikeja (at his send forth, March 1992).

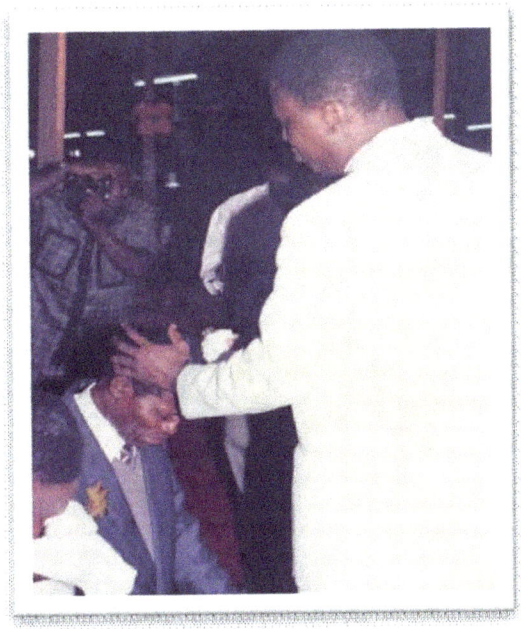

Abraham's Ordination as Full Pastor by Daddy E.A. Adeboye (Redemption Camp, August 1993).

Abraham's Ordination as Full Pastor - Group photograph with Daddy E.A. Adeboye (Redemption Camp, August 1993).

Ordination as Full Pastor - Abraham and Jane with Daddy Adetola and the Ogundipes (Redemption Camp, August 1993).

Abraham and Jane at home in Melbourne - as part of preparations towards "W@70" (Dec 2021).

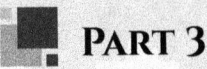

PART 3

ON A MISSION FOR JESUS

- 3.1 THE MANDATE

- 3.2 THE METHODS

- 3.3 THE MISTAKES

- 3.4 THE MEDALS

- 3.5 WELCOME TO PATMOS!

3.1

THE MANDATE

"^{18} *Jesus came and told his disciples, "I have been given all authority in heaven and on earth.* ^{19} *Therefore, go and make disciples of all the nations, baptizing them in the name of the Father and the Son and the Holy Spirit.* ^{20} *Teach these new disciples to obey all the commands I have given you. And be sure of this: I am with you always, even to the end of the age."* (Matthew 28:18-20 NLT)

A mandate is an authoritative command. Often, it comes from a higher or superior authority. The mandate for missions is an authoritative command. The authority (or Authorizer) of the mandate is God Himself (Matthew 28:18-20, Mark 16:15-18). It is a mandate "to go," and it begins with a genuine call to salvation. By God's grace, I experienced that on Wednesday 8th of July, 1981 - a few days to the end of the one-year mandatory National Youth Service Corps (NYSC) in Ondo State, South-West of Nigeria.

The next step of the mandate to me was to be a missionary. Several things led to that encounter and call.

Perhaps, and in retrospect, I can say that my service in God's vineyard began around mid-1983. I just changed my job (moving from the State Internal Revenue Board to the Administrative Cadre in the Lagos State Public Service).

The Lord laid it upon my heart to start a Lunch-Hour Fellowship at the Secretariat premises. I connected with other Christian brethren in the Secretariat, and the Fellowship began. However, the real Mandate came in May 1990, while I was in the UK - I was then a student at the University of Birmingham.

Background to the Call

Late in the preceding year, I had initiated a weekly Bible Study in my Student Hostel. The Fellowship had attracted other students from a wide range of nations - Africa (from West, East, South), the Caribbeans, Pacific Islands of Solomon Islands, Fiji, etc. Many times, a compassion that I could not explain would overwhelm me for people from East and mid-South Africa - particularly Kenyans, Ugandans, and South Africans. Their lifestyle of boozing, partying, and very loud music in such a civilized society, as Birmingham, bothered me a lot. So, I started to pray for them. Little did I know that it was the Holy Spirit's way of "apprehending" me. To cut a long story short, over the weekend of May 29th-31st May 1990, it became clear beyond any doubt that God was calling me to be a Missionary in East Africa!

It later became clear too that this burden was what God used to birth the call. It was as if God was saying "You are the one I will send to them!" I could relate better to Isaiah 6:8 (NLT), *"Then I heard the Lord asking, "Whom should I send as a messenger to this people? Who will go for us?" I said, "Here I am. Send me."* Based on this call, I started reading and making inquiries. One of the things I found out was that a missionary must have a home-based sending Church (or body). I also researched to find out about mission work in some nations in that region of Africa. Through the help of Pastor Phil Hill of Elim Church in Birmingham, I linked up with an elderly missionary in Tanzania. Eventually, I zeroed in on Zambia.

On returning to Nigeria in November 1990, I shared the call and the mandate with my spiritual father; Pastor Enoch Adeboye – The General Overseer of RCCG.

I later resigned from my job (as an Admin Officer) with the Lagos State Civil Service. On Wednesday, 1st April 1992, I became a full-time worker (along with my wife) in the Redeemed Christian Church of God (RCCG). On Friday 20th August 1993, God opened the way for us to leave Lagos, and go for mission work in Zambia.

At this juncture, I must chip in something very crucial in guiding my final decision. There was a man of God by the name, Rev. John Dansu (I thank God that He is still alive today). Rev. Dansu was a very senior civil servant but also a Spirit-filled Christian brother, and full of wisdom. On returning from Britain, I booked an appointment to see him about the call of God that I received, and how urgent it was. Then he asked me some questions and offered some counsel. He prayed with me, and I left his office. His advice guided my decision and helped me to smoothly withdraw my service from the State Government. On my own, if I had left earlier as I intended, it would have led to several complications (and possibly blackmail) of other Christians who may qualify for overseas staff development programs. We thank God that it is now over 30 Years that all these happened, and God has been very faithful on all fronts.

Challenges to the Call and the Mandate

These came on many fronts:

- First, from me! Giving up a Ph.D program was a huge decision. I had eyed myself holding a Ph.D degree in Development Economics, with all the promising opportunities of being a World Bank official!

- Then was the challenge of the future of our two very young children. In April 1992 when we entered fulltime ministry, these children were five and two-and half years old respectively. Looking back, my wife and I have every cause to be grateful to God. One of the reasons is that God did not let us go a begging any school principal or university registrar to give more time before paying school fees, etc. Today, both children are adults with post-graduate degrees. In addition, God also kept them (and us too) very healthy and free from every disease or infirmity. To God be all the glory.

- The third challenge came from my elder brothers. Some of whom felt we had gone to an extreme with our type of Christianity. I remembered one of them asked, "Are you okay?"

- The fourth challenge was from my workplace – from a loving boss who tried to dissuade me from answering God's call. He thought I had a great future in the State Public Service.

- Finally came the challenge from some brethren in the Church (RCCG VI/Ikoyi – our home-based local church) because the banking industry in Nigeria was undergoing some reforms, and great opportunities were emerging for new commercial, Microfinance and industrial banks to come up. These brethren were looking for reliable hands. So, when they heard that it was Development Finance that I studied, they requested me to join them to form banks, and also offered me reasonable positions and salary packages!

Challenges on the Call and the Mandate Itself

- The first has to do with how to relate with some Christian brothers. I found out that there were at least two classes of brethren in the Church (every Church or Ministry has the two classes):

* True brethren - Those who are reliable, but who may not see too far or see the big picture.

* False Brethren – these are Brothers who are false or are pretenders. One may point out that some of them started well, but they got corrupted along the line. Dealing or relating with them based on their past 'righteousness' can be disastrous!

- Another set of people I had to contend with were those who always wanted to have their own ways. This class of people seem to have a philosophy – *"It is either my way, or no way."* So, if they cannot have their ways, then everything must be grounded. Not just the work to be done, but even your own destiny!

The Sustaining Grace

In the situations described above, we have been sustained by God's grace, and a few principles:

- The assurance of the Call and Mandate – Knowing Who called, when, and where He called me.

- The fear of God - This made me always want to do what is right. It also made me want to do His will. I was not prepared to deliberately sin against God!

On one or two critical occasions, I have had to ask God to please step into the situation to prove that He truly called me, and in a very special way, He did!

Oshogbo, Osun State (Sept 1997) - Abraham with Predecessor - (Pastor A. A. Oludele) at Welcome/First Meeting of Area Pastors.

RCCG Osun State - Abraham and Jane with our Predecessors - Pst and Mrs A. A. Oludele (Sept 1997).

THE MANDATE

Pastoral visit/Church Foundation Laying, RCCG Ipetu-Modu, Osun Province I (1999)

Holy Ghost Rally (Akure, 2001)

Breakthrough Service with Daddy E. A. Adeboye (Akure, 2002).

Akure, Ondo State - CRFU Outreach - Abraham with Elders Felix and Jane Ohiwerei, and Dr Olusegun Mimiko (then State Commissioner for Health), 2002

Pastoral visit/Reception at RCCG Lagos Province 10, Region 2 (2008)

Pastoral visit/Church Dedication, Lagos Province 17, Region 2, Lagos (2008)

Abraham with Pastors Okey Mofunanya and Akintemi, Lagos (2008)

Abraham with Mummy Folu Adeboye (2009) opening of Region 2 Secondary school Lagos

Pastoral visit to RCCG (Palmgrove/Ilupeju Zone, Lagos Province 8) - Abraham with Zonal Pastor Adeolu Osunkeye, 2009

Pastoral visit to RCCG (Ajilete, Ese Odo, Ondo State - a Mission post of Lagos, Province 8, Somolu) - Abraham with Elder Elebiju being welcomed by Church Members (2009).

Pastoral visit to RCCG (Ajilete, Ese Odo, Ondo State - a Mission post of Lagos Province 8, Somolu) - Abraham with Elder Elebiju & Church Members (2009).

3.2

METHODS

"Timothy, my dear son, be strong through the grace that God gives you in Christ Jesus. ² You have heard me teach things that have been confirmed by many reliable witnesses. Now teach these truths to other trustworthy people who will be able to pass them on to others. ³ Endure suffering along with me, as a good soldier of Christ Jesus. ⁴ Soldiers don't get tied up in the affairs of civilian life, for then they cannot please the officer who enlisted them. ⁵ And athletes cannot win the prize unless they follow the rules." (2 Timothy 2:1-5)

Methods for ministry are (or should) derive from the mandate and the voice that gave the mandate. For every mandate God gives (or commissions), He has His methods of getting it fulfilled.

Regarding methods in ministry, two things are very critical:

- Knowing the mind of God.

- Having the right people around you (People we can call destiny helpers).

When one talks about the right people, God has His people everywhere. The truth however, is that the devil too has his agents everywhere (and in many cases, they will outnumber God's people)! In every assignment or new place, a critical prayer is to ask God to please always send His people to you.

Let me say this, when you arrive in a new place (or you are initiating a program or project), some people know that you are quite new, and that you are most likely to be in desperate need of helpers. So, they would be available to *"help"*, or to assist you. But in truth, they may be out to exploit you. Such people would try to pressurize you into committing too many things to their hands, and very quickly too. If you are not quick to discern, they may hold you to ransom or become a bottleneck to the purpose of God in the assignment.

Because our call or mandate in the main is in the area of foreign missions, I have had to be away from home on several occasions, especially when the children were growing up. One of them was born 3 days after I left Nigeria for the UK. By the time I returned, she was already more than 1 year old.

As part of that mercy which we enjoyed, God also gave us supportive brethren who were very helpful. Among them were Dr Femi and Mrs. Faith Odumade, Pastor Kayode

Osundahunsi, and many others. In addition, our Daddy and Mummy (The Adeboyes), in spite of their very tight schedule always checked on us.

It is important to point out here that on some occasions I did experience burn-out, and was at the risk of giving up. Some of the reasons were:

- Abandonment in the mission field.

- Betrayals by people.

- Persecutions for doing what is right. In many cases, such persecutions came from people whose ego and personal agenda were under threats!

- Distortions of truth for personal gains.

In all these, I thank God that He helped me to resort to Him who called me. Like David, *"I encouraged myself in the Lord."* (Hebrews 12:2; 1 Samuel 30:6c). On one occasion (in the mission field), God gave me a couple who became like a mother and father to me. On another occasion, the loneliness or abandonment was so much that to "feel at home", I had to go to the Nigerian High Commission in the Capital city of that country to relax.

Perhaps, it may be helpful to point out here that even though sin is a universal phenomenon, each country, region, and culture has its peculiarities (Jeremiah 17:9,

Romans 3:23). Where one may get worried is when a man or woman claims to be born again, and yet still acts like a non-believer. Hence, one needs a lot of patience, wisdom, and observation.

From all the foregoing, it may be wise for the younger generation of ministers and Missionaries (to among other things):

(a) Give priority to the Word of God

i. They should immerse themselves in the Word.

ii. They should let the Word of God rule their hearts.

iii. They should make the Word of God the final arbiter on all issues of their lives and ministry (Romans 12:1-2)

(b) They should always find out, and also stand for the truth (John 8:32, 36).

(c) They should quietly pursue their God-given mandate (Acts 10:35-35).

(d) They should always seek God's divine guidance and keep on track in all they needed to say, do, as well as where to go, and where not to go! God's Word had always been a lamp unto our feet, and a light unto our path (Psalm 119:105, 130).

Often, there is a mix-up on the "will" and the "mind" of God. There are definite and concrete differences between the two – the will and the mind of God. As one reads or studies the Bible, we discover the will of God (Psalm 119:105, 130). In Romans 12:1-2, the Bible made it clear that even with the will of God, there are three levels - His goodwill, His acceptable will, and His perfect will. Perhaps, one can also add the fourth - the permissive will of God. When you are heady and insist it is what you want that God must want, He will let you have it. However, there would be some consequences later!

When it comes to the "mind" of God, this involves two things. The first is receiving the mind of Christ (Philippians 2:5-8). One version of the Bible calls it the "attitude" of Christ. It means to be humble, obedient and focused on pleasing the Father. The other side of the "mind" of God has to do with having a very clear understanding of what He wants us to do, or where He wants us to go.

Now, to the main difference between the will and the mind of God. The will of God tells what God wants to be done (or what He would love to be done). But His mind lets us know when, where, and by what means He wants that thing done. The "means" can even be as detailed as God telling you the process, the procedure, as well as the people with whom He would get it done.

It is as we pray that God sheds more light on what He has revealed as His will. When this happens, then we will begin to discover the mind of God. Now, there are at least three main things to pay attention to when we talk about getting the mind of God:

- We need the help of the One who knows the mind of God - the HOLY SPIRIT (1 Corinthians 2:9-11).

- We also need a sanctified or renewed mind - (Romans 12: 1-2, John 17:17).

- Finally, we need an obedient heart. God reveals His mind only to those who will obey Him, no matter what He asked them to do! (Genesis 22:12-18, John 14:19).

It is to be noted that discovering the mind of God may take time. During such a period of waiting on God for His voice or direction, people may call you all sorts of names - they may say you are slow, foolish, inarticulate, toxic, wicked, negligent, etc. One thing is sure, when you secure divine direction and you obey it to the letter, it will pay off - even if people disagree, they won't be able to fault your action. By God's grace, I have several instances of this:

- Many times in choosing, appointing, or promoting people into positions, or transferring them, God had been our guide.

METHODS

- In a particular place we were transferred to, the Headquarter pastor just did what he liked. Every Sunday, he would welcome us to the Parish and thank us for visiting them. He would plan programs, print fliers with his own name, deliberately omitting my name. Thank God that he was at least courteous enough to put that of our Daddy (the General Overseer). To add insult to injury, this pastor would invite the one I took over from without my knowledge - we would meet only in the church. For two solid years, I left him there, but I kept on praying. One day, I just finished reading the Bible, and God brought a strange idea to my mind, *"Rearrange and make the place too small for him to stay!"* The Pastor was a Zonal Pastor. With God's wisdom, we made the Parish a Provincial Church, and got a Deacon (a Ph.D. holder, and who the big Pastor would not even ask to teach Sunday School), to act as the Parish Pastor. So, our friend was neatly transferred to another Zone. The result was a great peace. It also led to an explosive growth! It was later we began to hear of several financial misappropriations, and other things going on in the parish, prior to the time we effected the changes.

- There was also another case of a pastor who was doing what he liked. I just heard one morning, *"De-robe."* Before the week ran out, it became clear that God wanted me to suspend him, and I did. Even though he said I had no power to suspend him, it took the intervention of our Daddy, the General Overseer before he could be reinstated.

- Once I got to a new place, at the very first meeting I had (I think it was at a vigil before we were all to go in for the Service), I entered the office that was supposed to be my office, then the landlord (the most senior Zonal Pastor) said something in vernacular (Yoruba) - *"Let somebody go and get a seat for Baba")*! I just did as if I did not hear what he said. So, they got a seat for me in the corner of the room, and he conducted the affairs of the evening!

- In one place, a *"powerful"* man came to threaten me in the church office. He said (and I quote): "If they sent you here to come and investigate me, you are too small for that." He banged the table several times and stormed out of my office. In such a case, if you did not know who had called or sent you, you will shiver or run to the Toilet! Meanwhile, a particular word from the Lord about this man had come to us when we received the letter of transfer to the place. Humanly speaking, given what some of us saw on the surface, what God said about where we were going seemed unbelievable! Thank God that He is the Alpha and Omega. He is also the all-seeing, and all-knowing God.

Concerning the mind of God, the issue of timing is very critical. If we are not careful, one can be under pressure to go ahead of God and act. The result could be terrible. I remember in one mission field, my zeal to want to start an additional new branch of the church led me to make several efforts. However, for several months, there was no success. One day, I went to the same suburb where I had been going to look for space - this time for an entirely different purpose - to make more chairs for the main church. It was the Welder I was chatting with when, suddenly, the Lord opened my eyes and I saw space. After negotiating and paying him for the number of chairs we needed, I told him what I had been looking for in the area - a space where people could gather to watch a Christian film. The man said I could come and use his premises! Two weeks later, more than 200 people gathered to watch the film. Not too long after, a new branch of RCCG took off there. In fact, the man's wife became the choir leader at the place. I could go on and on. The truth is, God is still willing to direct us if we are willing to wait to know His will and mind. Glory be to God.

Let me conclude this section by adding that in the choice or appointment of people for assignments, God had long told us the priority factors to consider: *"Character above competence."* I found out that while competencies can easily be acquired, godly character is not easy to come by! Some people are highly competent, but they have serious character deficiency – they are morally bankrupt!

3.3

THE MISTAKES

The word mistake is defined as a wrong action attributable to bad judgment, ignorance, or inattention. A mistake is also said to be an understanding of something that is not correct. Thus, in life and ministry, mistakes may arise when we:

- Lack clarity of what to do.

- Lack the right timing in what we set out to do.

Over-trusting men, or trusting them too soon, and commit too much into their hands too early, could lead to costly mistakes in Ministry.

Often, we forget what the Word of God says in Jeremiah 17:9:

"the heart of men is deceitful and desperately wicked!"

As mistakes are part of the process of maturing leadership, I made some mistakes as a leader and some of these mistakes had impact on me and the work. Some of the mistakes, which I could also call challenges of ministry, include:

(i) Thinking that all who claim to be born-again or God's Children are truly so (Jeremiah 17:9).

(ii) Having to live and/or work with people who deliberately distort or read carnal meanings to the Word of God (meanings that God did not intend). For example,

"The Kingdom of God suffereth violence, and the violent take it by force" (Matthew 11:12). So, they are violent, they grab positions, blackmail leaders, lobby, etc.

- The gift of a man maketh a way for him (Proverbs 18:16). So, they bribe or buy their ways to the top through gifts, etc. More on this is discussed in the book, "The Third Epistle - A Leadership Reminiscence"

(iii) Perhaps another mistake I made which I did not realize until sometime later, was to assume that everything that a spirit-filled person says is totally and truly from the Holy Spirit. I realized along the line that there are at least about three spirits that can move a person to speak, act or react: the human spirit, the Spirit of God, and the spirit of Satan.

- Gad (a trusted spiritual adviser to King David), one day told the king to go ahead with the Temple Building project which the King had in mind. He assured, King David that God was 100% pleased with the project. Later, God convicted the Seer to the contrary, and he ran back to the king that what he told him earlier was wrong, but that it was David's son who would build the Temple.

- Peter, (in Matthew 16:15-19, 21-23) made an astounding statement to the extent that the Lord Jesus had to declare *"...flesh and blood has not revealed this to you, but My Father who is in heaven..."* Almost immediately, another spirit sneaked in and began to speak through Peter. Thank God, the Master Jesus recognized the spirit, and rebuked it (rather than rebuking Peter) - Matthew 16:21-23.

Among other things, over the years, God also taught me:

(i) To be careful with human beings – I learned not to take people just at face value (some products have a good packaging, but little value is found on the inside)

(ii) Not to move or act until I have clarity of what to do – There is a need to wait for divine direction – no matter how long it takes. By "Divine" here, it includes directives from the leader above or who sent me.

Even though there are mistakes one would wish are not repeated, it is possible to keep on repeating them. For example, in a particular mission field, I opened up too much to two men on how I felt about a particular man, and it backfired seriously. The two men went to tell their kinsman (who is not a true believer) everything I told them, and they put me in the middle!

Also, I found out that I tend to easily trust people. Some of these people I found, in the long run, are not trustworthy! This has been a great challenge! There were two instances of this: On one occasion, I went all out to recommend a 'Brother' for an appointment. On another, I guaranteed a 'Brother' for a huge project loan. Both of them unfortunately abused the privilege as well as my generosity.

One of the challenges of ministry, and perhaps of leadership is placing people in leadership roles based on their ability and gifting only to find out later that they lack integrity and character!

To correct this anomaly, God had helped me among other things to:

i. Pray for divine intervention.

ii. Keep my eyes on them to prevent more serious damage.

iii. Minimize their sphere of influence.

In addition, we had ensured a constant flow of correct information to the people such negative leaders might want to negatively influence.

To avoid the recurrent problem of *"success in leadership without a successor"*, there are a few things that successful leaders must pay attention to. These include:

- Recruitment – Leaders should have a selection process that identifies and picks the best available hand. Even here, there is a need to be sensitive to the Holy Spirit.

- Leaders should have a clear career and growth path, as well as a well-structured training and development program that each staff must go through before moving up in the system.

- Leaders should not promote people just because they have spent some years.

- Very importantly, and for senior management positions, people should go round critical units of the organization before being moved high up.

- Finally, it is very critical to adhere to agreed organizational policies.

In all, two things have continued to be the driving principles behind all I do in life and ministry:

a) The mercy of God and the willingness to please Him as a matter of priority - knowing that I will one day stand to give account to Him.

b) God is the One Who will do the Final marking.

(Romans 14:12, Revelations 22:10-12). In addition, a determination to seek the good of the organization – in as much as it aligns with Kingdom interests – has also helped me.

To the *young and aspiring leaders wanting to be successful in leadership,* I will advise that they should:

- Have a clear vision, and strong focus.

- Aspire to be men and women of godly character.

- Learn to persevere.

- Pray and ask God to send them destiny helpers.

Let me conclude this chapter by emphasizing that every assignment has its ups and downs. There are what can be likened to "industrial hazards" to the call into ministry, and missions in particular. The ones I experienced are of two categories: job-related, as well as environmental.

As a missionary (with a Nigerian complex or mentality), I had a lot of culture shocks when I got to my first mission station (in Zambia, East Africa). In Nigeria, mothers back babies i.e. they carry babies on their back. In Zambia, mothers put the baby in a basket-like bag in front! It was later I understood why.

Another of my experience had to do with the death of infants or babies. In Nigeria, even though we mourn the death of babies and infants, we don't take it as so serious a phenomenon that makes it as if the whole world would end because a baby died! One day, I was invited to come and conduct the funeral service for a 3-months old baby girl that died.

With the benefit of hindsight, there are some things that I would do differently if I have to. For instance, my attitude to the WORD – the Holy Bible – if I had read it more or meditated and knew earlier what I now know in, and about the Word, I would certainly have done many things far better – in life, at home, and in ministry.

3.4

THE MEDALS

"9 Whenever the living beings give glory and honor and thanks to the one sitting on the throne (the one who lives forever and ever), 10 the twenty-four elders fall down and worship the one sitting on the throne (the one who lives forever and ever). And they lay their crowns before the throne and say, 11 "You are worthy, O Lord our God, to receive glory and honor and power. For you created all things, and they exist because you created what you pleased." (Revelation 4:9-11 NLT)

Let me begin by saying that if there is anything that can be referred to as success in ministry, we should learn to return all the glory to God. He is the ONE who created and preserved us; He also is the One who saved us, called us, and had been backing us up over the years. Without Him, I, in particular, would have been dead many times over. He is the PILLAR that holds my life. He is the One who has been my stay (Psalm 89:1, 22-24, Isaiah 41:10-16, Luke 10:19).

Two ways He has been of utmost help are in the areas of *His Presence*, and the aspect of *His guidance* - especially through His Written Word (the Bible), as well as through His Holy

Spirit. The Word of God – the HOLY BIBLE is my main source of life. But for the Bible, life marriage, and ministry would have been miserable! I give God all the glory. The Word of God has saved me from several troubles. I mean real troubles. It has also healed me, and built my relationships (both at home and in ministry).

On many occasions, I have had to depend on the light I got from the Word of God and the Holy Spirit for appropriate words to speak or actions to take. For example, even though I have heard, and even used the word 'discretion' several times before, it was through the Bible that the term *Discretion* came to me more vividly, and I started looking for its real meaning. I later discovered or realized that there were so many cases of discretion in the Bible.

God has also always been very gracious to send us destiny helpers, and *"king makers,"* wherever He sent us to. With time and prayers, He has always linked us with them.

It is crucial to learn to give all the glory to God for whatever we achieve in life. God is the Enabler (Isaiah 42: 8, Philippians 2:13, John 15:5, Genesis 32:10). To refuse to give God all the glory can be very dangerous! Among other things, we will be limiting ourselves! Also, God can withdraw and leave you to it. When He does, you will begin to make serious and avoidable mistakes. More importantly, are the lessons to learn from the story of King Nebuchadnezzar (in Daniel 4:1-end).

Perhaps some of the reasons that could make mortal men refuse to credit their accolades to their Maker and Creator are:

- Pure ignorance – Ignorance of who we are, in relation to God.

- Deception of the devil – Making a human being feel he/she is something when in truth he is zero without God.

Zambia (January 1994) - One-Day Leadership Orientation Workshop - held at first RCCG Parish, Akanongo Road, Olympia Extension, Lusaka.

Abraham with Bro Peter and Sis Theresa Chanda (my immediate and very faithful Assistants at the first RCCG Parish in Lusaka Zambia), 1994.

First Pastoral visit to RCCG Perth, Western Australia (April, 2011).

First Pastoral visit to RCCG Perth, Western Australia (April, 2011) - stressing a point at Workers and Ministers' Meeting.

Welcoming Daddy E. A. Adeboye and Mummy Folu Adeboye to PNG (2013)

Pastoral visit to RCCG (Honiara, Solomon Islands) - Abraham (on arrival) with Pst Joseph Olawale and his Protocol Team, 2015

Pastoral visit to RCCG (Palau 2016) - Abraham with Pst Cyprian Adaba at an interdenominational Youth Meeting (organized by AOG Church, Palau).

Pastoral visit to RCCG Western Australia (2016)

Pastoral visit to RCCG (Palau 2016) - Abraham with Church members

Abraham & Jane with Pastors @ inauguration of RCCG Jesus Court, Newcastle, Australia (2017)

Pastoral visit to RCCG (Guam 2017) - Abraham conducting a One-Day Workers and Ministers' Leadership Workshop.

Pastoral visit to RCCG (Guam 2017) - Abraham with pastor Rob Paulinho and Church members.

Pastoral visit to RCCG Vanuatu (Victory House, Hdq in Port Vila) - Abraham with Church leaders (just before departing for Australia)

 I AM ABRAHAM

Pastoral visit to RCCG (Suva, Fiji) - Abraham with SOD Graduands, 2017.

Pastoral visit to RCCG (Samoa, 2017) - Abraham received at Airport by Sis Amelia & Bro Houlton Faasau, with two of their children.

Abraham & Jane on Mission

Abraham on Mission

3.5

WELCOME TO PATMOS[3]

Towards the end of our Church's 59th Annual Convention (August 2010), I got a letter posting me out of Nigeria to a place that had been variously described as "down and under," "ends of the earth," "no man's land," etc. However, as time went on, God made me realize that it was a land of inheritance, a land of possession, and the land of blessing. Geographically, I realize that rather than being the "end of the earth," the place was indeed the beginning. From there the sun rises 10 hours ahead of Nigeria, and 17 hours ahead of Texas (USA). Also, and like I told some people some time ago since in this same part of the world we see and enter each New Year ahead of many countries by the same number of hours, by that token we could be seeing our Lord Jesus at His soon second coming, 10-17 Hours ahead of Nigeria and Texas!

In life and ministry, God has been kind and faithful to send me helpers of destiny, particularly wherever He sent us to. Such people had played vital roles in my life that it is only Heaven that can reward them. The posting under discussion here was not my first of being sent out, both locally and overseas, on ministry assignments. However, this was unique in many senses. The greatest help in life and ministry so far had been what God had stored up and awaiting my arrival in AUSPAC. The blessing had been both spiritual, physical, and emotional.

The utmost joy I derive (and I'm still deriving) in this posting is the fact that God has used it to draw me a little closer to Himself. More than ever, I see and hear Him more clearly. For this, I am most grateful to God, and my leaders. No money can buy this!

In one of his prison notes, the man of God, Richard Wurmbrand, said *"Being alone is the prerequisite for plumbing into your own depths. I would be much alone, aloof from you, most dearly beloved, even if I were not in prison."* In John 14:28, 31 Jesus had to leave the world (including friends, relations, and even His foes) so He could go to His Father *"that the world may know that I love the Father."* He also said, *"I will no longer talk much with you because I go to My Father"* (John 14:30). There is, therefore, the need to be WISE (as a man, a husband, a parent, a pastor, or a counselor).

By wisdom here, I mean being wise enough to learn to depart (alone) into the Father's presence to know Him more, contemplate your depths, and discover hidden and ultimate truths!

Another of the benefits of being in this part of the Lord's harvest field is that friends and enemies alike don't disguise. At home, especially for a relatively senior officer like me, and operating in a large organization like ours, it is really hard to know who is a friend, and who is an enemy. People love and or hate you for official reasons.

Often, you can be loved for what people hope to get from you in terms of favors – whether duly or unduly. You can also be loved out of fear - fear of what you have the power to do to them by virtue of your position, or perceived influence.

In the same vein, you can be hated for what you stand for if you will not let men have their way, or allow them to exploit the loopholes and weaknesses of the system. Your insistence on righteous standards and due diligence are enough to make you a sworn enemy of many.

The situation in the mission field is quite different. You can easily relatively know your true friends as well as real enemies. In His Sovereignty, God has the power to turn enemies into friends and to arrest unrepentant enemies. In Psalm 89:22-24 (KJV), among several promises, God told David:

"22 The enemy shall not exact upon him; nor the son of wickedness afflict him. 23 And I will beat down his foes before his face, and plague them that hate him. 24 But my faithfulness and

my mercy shall be with him: and in my name shall his horn be exalted." (Please also see Isaiah 41:10-16)

Still talking about my "Patmos" experience, it also dawned on me that there are very few true friends among humans. The ONLY true and genuine friend is Jesus (Proverbs 18:24, John 15:13, Romans 5:8).

Finally, being located in this part of the world gives me the conviction that in a way that is beyond human calculations, God was fulfilling in me the words of our Lord Jesus in Matthew 28:18-20, particularly verse 20b: *"...and lo, I am with you always, even unto the end of the world. Amen"*

Deep within me, I knew that *'The I AM That I AM'* is always with me – whether I feel it or not. I knew He is very close - even closer than my shadows. It did not matter if the journey I was embarking upon is on the ground, in the air, or on the high seas of the Pacific Islands of PNG, Vanuatu, Solomon Islands, Fiji, Samoa, American Samoa, New Zealand, or those on the West like Palau, Guam, Saipan, Pohnpei, etc.

I perceived too that *'till the end of the world'* could mean at least two things – both geography, space, or time. That is, when I finish my race on the earth, or He returns to take me to glory for my reward (1 John 3:1-3, Revelation 22:10-12).

Pastoral visit to RCCG (Guam 2017) - Abraham with Pst Jack and Sukiriyam Stogdill

Abraham @ SOD Graduation Perth, WA (2017)

Abraham and Jane Haastrup - Melbourne City - as part of preparations for Daddy GO's 2018 Visit

Pastoral visit to RCCG Fiji (2017) - Abraham with Daddy Joseph Obayemi (National Overseer for Nigeria) and Pst Jerry Waqanaibete

PART 4

THE VOICE AND VALUES OF DESTINY

| 4.1 | THE VOICE OF DESTINY |

| 4.2 | THE VOICE TO ME AND FOR ME |

| 4.3 | LIFE-SHAPING VALUES AND PRINCIPLES |

| 4.4 | PUSHED INTO DESTINY |

| 4.5 | LIVING TESTIMONIES |

| 4.6 | ONCE, I WAS YOUNG |

4.1

THE VOICE OF DESTINY

An indisputable fact of life is that it is one thing for a destiny to be ordained, yet another to have it fulfilled. Many people are known to have a glorious destiny laid out before them. Some even discover and make efforts to fulfill it. However, along the line, some things happen, and a glorious destiny gets derailed, diverted, and ultimately destroyed. May yours never be like that in Jesus' name.

There is a voice that can destroy destiny. There is also a voice that shapes and straightens a man's destiny. A voice has been variously described as the faculty of utterance; an instrument or medium of expression. It is also said to be a wish, a choice, or an opinion openly or formally expressed, a right of expression, an influential power.

As a medium of expression, a voice can be spoken, heard, or unheard. This means a voice can be audible or inaudible. It can also come from various sources. There is the voice of man - friends, loved ones, enemies, adversaries, and foes. Such may be regenerated or unregenerated men. There is the voice of Satan and those of his agents - demons, systems (and one may include here some aspects of the media, etc.). Of course, and most importantly, there is the voice of God (Lamentations 3:37).

Whether audible or inaudible, heard or unheard, voices influence or impact our daily lives, and those of our loved ones. Some voices edify and build us up - they encourage us and inspire our faith. On the other hand, some voices discourage, tear down, create fear, and destroy our faith!

God speaks in diverse ways. In my Book, God Still Speaks Today (Almond Tree, 1993), this subject had been dealt with exhaustively. One of the primary ways God speaks is through His Word - the written Word (the Holy Bible). He also speaks through His Living Word - Jesus Christ (Hebrews 1:1-3). Of course, God speaks through His Holy Spirit. God also speaks through His servants (2 Chronicles 20:20), and several other mediums and circumstances.

God's voice and /or words are very powerful! (Hebrews 4:12, John 6:63, Psalms 119:105, 130, Isaiah 55:10-11). God's voice is both creative and restorative. His voice and word can heal, deliver, set free, and change situations. It can change death to life, grave to glory, and emptiness to fullness. His voice gives direction (Psalm 33:10, John 1:3-4, Mark 5:21-24, 35-43, Luke 7:11-17, John 11:38-44), etc. The voice of the Lord can also locate and re-relocate (Exodus

3:1-15).

In Lamentations 3:37, the Bible made it clear that God's voice is a needed priority for and to every man. It can make a huge difference between life and death. His voice is to be made the first-ever to be heard every morning. When you hear Him, you need to also believe what He says. There is a need to let His voice shape your heart, your day, and your life. It is wise to let what He says, particularly about you, rule your ways. Whatever anyone else says is secondary. For example, maybe you wake up one morning, and God said to you through His Word or His Holy Spirit, telling you as in Isaiah 41:10-13 (KJV), that:

"10 Fear thou not; for I am with thee: be not dismayed; for I am thy God: I will strengthen thee; yea, I will help thee; yea, I will uphold thee with the right hand of my righteousness. 11 Behold, all they that were incensed against thee shall be ashamed and confounded: they shall be as nothing; and they that strive with thee shall perish. 12 Thou shalt seek them, and shalt not find them, even them that contended with thee: they that war against thee shall be as nothing, and as a thing of nought. 13 For I the LORD thy God will hold thy right hand, saying unto thee, Fear not; I will help thee."

Then maybe someone walked in (and that someone could be your spouse, your father, mother, etc.) to your bedroom and said to you, *"You are a fool,"* or *"You are senseless,"* and probably that *"You are a failure."* Don't let that enter your heart and trouble you! Let the more assuring "First Voice" give peace and confidence to your soul. On the same day, you may get to your workplace, and your boss, senior colleague, or even a jealous co-worker may harass you in some way. Don't let all these shake or destabilize you. What God has spoken is superior!

The truth is that, whether to you as a person or to circumstances and issues around you, when God has not spoken every other voice is just filling space. Of course, when God has spoken, you don't need any other voice. Just obey and your miracle is certain - it is a matter of time (Numbers 23:19, Romans 4:17-21).

4.2

THE VOICE TO ME AND FOR ME

"¹⁰ It was the Lord's Day, and I was worshiping in the Spirit Suddenly, I heard behind me a loud voice like a trumpet blast. ¹¹ It said, "Write in a book everything you see, and send it to the seven churches in the cities of Ephesus, Smyrna, Pergamum, Thyatira, Sardis, Philadelphia, and Laodicea." ¹² When I turned to see who was speaking to me, I saw seven gold lampstands." (Revelation 1:10-12 NLT)

If God had not been real or been alive, and if God's being alive is not evidenced by His speaking, and being heard, someone like me would have either been dead a long time ago, or would have gone berserk, and nakedly roaming the streets of some cities! But glory be to God (John 16:33).

By "the voice to me and for me," I am talking about the voice of God – both spoken and heard – verbally in my ears, or my heart as I meditated in the written Word of God (the Holy Bible). Most of these encounters happened through inspiration or conviction received that brought peace to my heart, and later confirmed by the Scriptures.

The Bible, through Prophet Isaiah, had earlier said in Isaiah 26:3-4; *"You will keep him in perfect peace, Whose mind is stayed on You, Because he trusts in You. Trust in the Lord forever, For in Yah, the Lord, is everlasting strength."*

Through His Word and the Holy Spirit, God has been helping me to have a deep understanding of who He – the Almighty God is – especially the interplay of His awesome power in the universe. Also, through His Word and His Holy Spirit, God has been giving me some understanding of human beings - Believers and Unbelievers alike. The main or dominant voice that, by God's grace, has manifestly been directing or leading me in life is that of God.

With time, hearing God's voice has become relatively easier, especially after immersing myself in God's Word. The sanctifying power of God's Word makes our heart receptive to the voice of God (Romans 12:1-2, John 17:17).

Also, during Praise and Worship (either personal or corporate), as well as in times of prayers, I have learned to tune my ears and mind to Heaven for God's Word to me, and for me (Jeremiah 1:4-5).

Over the years, it became very clear to me that my peace, my progress in life, and indeed my overall destiny are all strictly tied to God - His Written Word, and my knowing and obeying His very voice (which I have since been referring to as "The First Voice"). Whenever God helped me to know His mind, or what He was saying to me, and also helped me to obey Him, the result had added value to my life. On the other hand, anytime I, for whatever reason, disobeyed, I always ran into problems some of which had been to some extent, of very devastating consequences!

4.3

LIFE-SHAPING VALUES AND PRINCIPLES

I am grateful for the great mercy of God that brought me into salvation through the Lord Jesus. Another precious thing I can never be grateful enough to God for is the access He has given me to His Word - the Holy Bible. It is the greatest book, and it has been my mainstay over the years. Scriptures such as Acts 10:34-35, Luke 10:19, Psalm 89:1, 22-24, Romans 8:28, etc. among others have helped me both daily and in very critical times.

As I stated earlier in this book, it became clear that there is a redemptive purpose in each of the names given to me at birth. In particular, the name Abraham has become more than just a name but a destiny link!

This chapter focuses on the second of the two very related issues in my life that had combined to shape my life and destiny: the Voice, as well as the principles and values. Both had been used by God over the years to sustain me in the journey of life. Having already discussed the Voice, I now move to look at the principles and values.

By principles and values, I mean my personal codes of right conduct which God has helped me to develop and live by over the years, especially since I came to know Jesus Christ as personal Saviour and Lord. The principles and values also include my own personal standards of judging what and what are important in life.

I came to realize that as individuals or organisations, it is not enough to list out or talk about principles and core values, they must be lived out for others in our sphere of influence to see, if they will take us seriously, and even emulate us!

For ease of reference, and to help the understanding of readers, I have grouped the various experiences discussed here into five:

1. Word-based principles and values.

2. Intuition-based principles and values.

3. Reflection-based principles and values.

4. Challenge-based principles and values.

5. Attitude-based principles and values.

Word-based Principles and Values

(i) Knowledge and fear of God – These prevented me from taking God for granted. Over time, it dawned on me that God is too big to play games with. Also that no one can be too clever with God. God is obviously not a frivolous or an ambiguous God!

"32Those who do wickedly against the covenant he shall corrupt with flattery; but the people who know their God shall be strong, and carry out great exploits....23Thus says the Lord: "Let not the wise man glory in his wisdom, Let not the mighty man glory in his might, Nor let the rich man glory in his riches; 24But let him who glories glory in this, That he understands and knows Me, That I am the Lord, exercising loving-kindness, judgment, and righteousness in the earth. For in these I delight," says the Lord. (Daniel 11:32, Jeremiah 9:23-24).

(ii) The reality and vivid fulfilments of some particular guiding scriptures: For example, Exodus 14:14, Psalm 89:1, 22-24, Luke 10:19, Acts 10:34-35, Romans 8:32, 1 Chronicles 4:9-10, Isaiah 40:3-5; 41:10-16); among others.

Truly, God is no respecter of persons, any man in any nation who will fear Him and do what is right in His eyes will be accepted by Him. Also, if God did not spare Jesus, He won't spare any man! Hence, I (and no one for that

matter), should ever over-flog God's mercy and covenant (Gen. 17:9, Isaiah 40:8, 1 Kings 11:1-11, Proverbs 1:24-33).

Intuition-based Principles and Values

(i) Getting direction from God when I have a preaching and teaching ministry, or assignments. Some of the principles I follow include:

First, I thank God for the privilege of life, and for the assignment at hand. Then, I begin to read the relevant Scriptural passages on the subject. I also take time to ask God specifically for His mind on the matter – for the people who will hear the Word– hence, I coined the phrase: "the Word to me and for me". I ask God for His Word to them (and for them). I also ask for His presence and backing as I go for any ministry assignment.

(ii) While in prayer and or worship, or when studying the Word of God, God has taught me to listen in my heart, and tune my ears to Heaven and to His Holy Spirit. Through this act, God passes to me divine ideas, instructions as well as warnings. Recently too, God extended this grace to times when I am in "ordinary" conversations with people. I try to be in tune with Heaven. At such times, the spirit operating in the person with whom I am discussing often get exposed. This helps me to weigh or assess the person as well as what he or she may be saying -

whether giving advice, bringing some suggestions, or even looking for a fault, or they were out to pick offenses or make a request.

(iii) In my personal (or private) and official or ministry life, in as much as God helped me, I have based my words of counsel, as well as policy advice on the light I receive from the Word of God, His Holy Spirit, and evidence available - especially from trends in the Scriptures (the laws of precedence, and harvest). Based on all these, if those around me (be they colleagues, subordinates, or superiors), reject, ignore, or even castigate or call me names, I don't quarrel. However, I try to do three things:

- Pray for them and myself.

- I look forward to the outcomes.

- I count on the great element of time, as well as God's faithfulness (to honor His Word).

Reflection-based Principles and Values

These are observations and trends from the Scriptures, people, and events.

(i) Recognizing who God is in my life, and giving His Word priority place, and attention.

(ii) Knowing what God has called me to do, and sticking to it. Those who criticize me today will copy me tomorrow when they begin to see God's faithfulness. Also included here are personal experiences that reinforced Scriptures, and taught me some lasting lessons, or changed my attitude.

(iii) The discovery and belief in God's dual laws of precedence and harvest.

(iv) Resource management (Time or Money, etc. - Tithing ALL)

(v) While I must live by facts, however, I realize that not all facts are true. Hence, in between facts, I should learn to DISCERN THE TRUTH (John 8:32, 36).

(vi) On offenses within the Body of Christ (especially from fellow brethren), I came to the truth that not all who profess to be saved are genuine Christian Brothers! Hence, Apostle Paul's admonition in 2 Timothy 2:19-26 (NLT), had helped me a lot:

"[19]But God's truth stands firm like a foundation stone with this inscription: "The lord knows those who are his," and "All who belong to the lord must turn away from evil." [20] In a wealthy home some utensils are made of gold and silver, and some are made of wood and clay. The expensive utensils are used for special occasions, and the cheap ones are for everyday use. [21] If

you keep yourself pure, you will be a special utensil for honorable use. Your life will be clean, and you will be ready for the Master to use you for every good work. ²² Run from anything that stimulates youthful lusts. Instead, pursue righteous living, faithfulness, love, and peace. Enjoy the companionship of those who call on the Lord with pure hearts. ²³Again I say, don't get involved in foolish, ignorant arguments that only start fights. ²⁴A servant of the Lord must not quarrel but must be kind to everyone, be able to teach, and be patient with difficult people. ²⁵ Gently instruct those who oppose the truth. Perhaps God will change those people's hearts, and they will learn the truth. ²⁶Then they will come to their senses and escape from the devil's trap. For they have been held captive by him to do whatever he wants."

(vii) Salvation - The purpose of salvation is not to make a person live on earth perpetually, or forever. Rather, it is to help the one who is saved to live right and please God and be able to maximize the number of days/years that God in HIS Sovereignty has allocated to him or her. Wickedness and wrong living, will obviously shorten a man's life! (Isa 57:21; Ezek33:11-12).

(viii) Redemptive gifts - Recognizing, developing, and using them. One of the gifts I realized that I seem not to have had much of, is speaking eloquently or with oratory power. Notwithstanding this, I was active at

literary and debating society in my Secondary School days. On the other hand, it appeared that God had generously given me a great gift - the ability to write! By the time somebody sits near me for about five minutes, he or she would note this. I can write on any piece of paper irrespective of its size - no paper is too small for me to write upon! God also helps me to keep records of divine inspirations.

This special gift or grace, had opened me to several assignments and positions. Because people observe or realize that I do write or make notes, they readily suggest my name as Secretary to committees, associations, etc. More than twice, for two Committees to which I was initially appointed as Secretary (or Assistant Secretary), I eventually rose to become Chairman.

(ix) Sowing and reaping - Everyman (either knowingly or unknowingly) is at one point or the other sowing or reaping something! The great man of God, Evangelist Billy Graham gave a testimony of a visit he made to a prison. There, he saw an old man sobbing profusely. The Evangelist enquired why the man was crying. The prison warden told him that the man wasn't just weeping, he was in fact reaping! The only thing that can prevent evil reaping is to restitute our ways. Through restitutions, we uproot the evil we had earlier sown or planted.

(x) The Law of Precedence - While there is no place in the Bible where this particular law was written, it is clear that it is a valid spiritual law. The law simply says that if any person did something in the Bible, whether good or evil, the results (be it a reward or punishment), that such a person got will also be the same for anyone who does the same, even today! (Malachi 3:6, Acts 10:34-35, Isaiah 40:8).

(xi) There is no single person that God has not given gifts or talents. In the same way, everyone is prone to abuse, misuse, ignore, or refuse to develop or use his or her gifts - if not disciplined and sensitive to GOD, the giver.

(xii) The brothers of Joseph (Genesis 37:23-25) - They kidnapped and threw their very brother (Joseph) into a cistern! One day, the curiosity of imagination caught me, and I began to see them grab Joseph, blindfold him, strip him naked, and then throw him into the cistern. Perhaps Joseph landed head first, back or on his neck! I believe, however, that the same God who restrained the brothers from killing Joseph must have landed him safely on his two feet. Unconcerned about what may have happened to Joseph, the brothers sat down and were still able to eat - as if nothing grievous had happened!

 I AM ABRAHAM

Today, there are many so-called *"Brothers of Joseph"*, whether in the family, in the office, in business, and of course in the church. They can cast you into the cistern, and then sit to eat - unconcerned whether you are dead or alive.

(xiii) I have met some people who are apt to correct or reprimand you for minute misdeeds. However, if you dare attempt to point out their obvious fault, or correct them, they will immediately take a trip to the archives and pull out your file. You can imagine the rest of what may follow – they can even abuse you to your third and fourth generation!

(xiv) There is the possibility in life to be lied against, and even be punished for an offense one may not have committed. The good news is that if we stick to God, and godliness, even in that very unusual situation, God will come through for us. The story of Joseph particularly illustrates this. The wife of his Master lied against him, and he was thrown into prison without investigation that could have established the truth. From the same prison, Joseph was brought to Pharaoh who later appointed Joseph as his second in command! Also worthy of note in this story is the lesson that if and when someone who used to trust in, and rely on you suddenly turns his or her face away from you, or even "imprisons" you or send you into exile, don't be troubled. God may have allowed it. He may be using the experience to prepare you for your next level, or to get you nearer your destiny! Imagine if Potiphar had not thrown Joseph into prison. He would not have met Pharaoh's Chief Baker and Chief Butler whose dreams Joseph decoded. It was the Chief Butler who later told Pharaoh that he met a man in prison who accurately interpreted their dreams. That was what launched Joseph into the limelight.

(xv) Isaiah 26:10-11 - No matter how much good God does to some people, there is an evil in men that will always provoke them to think and do evil! If a man can do this to God - the ALMIGHTY ONE, how much less to fellow men. So, I minimize my resources of time and energy towards such people. However, I include them in my prayers that God will touch their hearts (2 Tim. 2:24-26, NLT).

(xvi) Romans 8:28 - Before all things can work together for the good of man, it must first have worked for the good of God Himself. That is, it must first align with God's plan, purpose, and glory. Added or connected to this verse, is Daniel 11:32c. If you truly know your God, and you are convinced that ALL things work together for your good, it means no man or situation can hold you to ransom for too long.

(xvii) Succession/arriving in a new place - God and experience had taught me that:

(a) When I arrive in a new place of posting, it is not everyone who comes to welcome me enthusiastically into the new place that is sincere. With time, each one's true color will begin to show forth. However, there is the possibility of a positive change of heart.

For instance, on arrival to the land of the Gadarene, Jesus was first met by a man with several unclean spirits. Jesus dislodged the demons from the man's life, and he (the man), later became a mighty Evangelist, to the extent that the whole ten cities in the territory heard about the transforming power of Jesus! (see Mark 5:1-20).

(b) I have learned not to make changes so soon on arrival. Even though I make it clear at the onset that things would not continue as before - simply because my predecessor and I were two different personalities; but particularly because if the authorities of the organization wanted things to continue as before they would not initiate transfers or promotion, etc.

(xviii) Isaiah 28:13: God is a teacher. I mean GOD - the Trinity. Here, God the Father is referred to as the greatest teacher. Jesus too is a great teacher - often, His Disciples referred to Him as 'Rabbi' (The Great Teacher). The Holy Spirit also is a teacher. Jesus called Him the teacher who will teach us all things that He (Jesus) could not teach us. The Isaiah text mentioned here tells us how God the Father teaches - line by line, one at a time. One version of the Bible described it as *"precept by precept."* This discovery led me to the "spiritual reading of the Scriptures"[4]

It brought me to a new dimension of understanding the Word of God - the Holy Bible.

(xix) In Acts 10:34-35, we read *"... God is no respecter of persons, but in every nation, anyone who fears Him and does what is right in His eyes will be acceptable to Him."* 1 Kings 11:1-11, and Isaiah 29:1-3 are two of the several instances in the Bible where God demonstrated that, truly, He is no respecter of persons. These particular instances should alert any man, and tell him never to dare take God for granted! In Isaiah 29:1-3, God (and not the Devil), was the One talking. He said He would be an enemy to Jerusalem - His very city! God said further that He would attack her walls and also build siege towers, and ultimately destroy the city. Now, in Jerusalem, there is a high point - the temple and the altar. If God, due to the sins of His people (the Israelites) could destroy His city that contains His own House (His earthly palace and throne, with the priests in it), then truly He is no respecter of persons! Have you been taking the Word of God for granted? It is high time you repented (Proverbs 1:24-33).

Challenge-based Principles and Values

One of the benefits of the challenges we face in life is that they push us towards God – we run to Him through His Word – the Holy Bible, and in prayer.

(I) Talking about prayers, we all need to grow in or improve our prayer life.

As Christians, part of the challenges we have in the place of prayer include not knowing what to pray about. At the base of this may be the fact that we don't study the Scriptures. If and when we study God's Word, prayer points must of necessity emerge. In God's Word, we would get a lot of prayer points - either something to thank God for, or something to ask for from Him - for ourselves, for others, or for His Kingdom.

While not claiming to be a strong prayer warrior, one of the ways God has helped me is through a particular praying format known as *"Praying the Alphabet."* The Alphabet A-Z are used to pray on each day of the month. For example:

1 2 3 4 5 6 7 8 9 10 11 12 13 14…22 23 24 25 26

A B C D E F G H I J K L M N O…V W X Y Z

As you wake up each day of the month, you can ask the Holy Spirit to drop specific words, names (of people and places), or situations and challenges, etc., in your heart. It will be very helpful to have a journal you can write or record God's instructions on. On 'A' days, for instance, you may have something like this:

A - Aa Ab Ac Ad Ae Af Ag Ah Aj Ak…Ax Az

Aa - Aaron,

Aba - Abandon Abb Abe Abh Abi Abj…. Abs

Abj – Abject,

Abl – Ablast, Ablaze,

Abo - Aborigine; About; above,

Abr - Abraham,

Abs - Absalom, Absence/absentee; Absolute; Absolve; Abstinence; etc.

(ii) Isaiah 29:4 - When people speak or talk, it is important to try and listen! A lot of things could determine what people say. For example, they may be speaking from their location - physical, mental, emotional, financial, and/or spiritual locations. Thus, a good knowledge of their location may help us to empathize with them. Such knowledge will also help us to be reflective rather than being reflexive.

Some people speak deep from the earth - they speak from the terrible, nasty, traumatic experience they have had in life. Perhaps, they have been betrayed, manipulated, or denied some rights. They may also have been abused, violated. Some people also speak out of a wide or deep knowledge of the complexities of the system of the world - its economy, its politics, international diplomacy, and conspiracy theories. It is obvious, too, that until some people get to the deep of the earth, until they become zero or even get below zero (to minuses), or come to the end of all their wits, they will never accept that they need help; they won't look up or call upon God for help (Psalm 107:15-20).

Attitude-based Principles and Values

(i) The conviction that I am not an accident of nature - God has a purpose, a plan, and a place for me in life. Hence,

- there is no need to hurry and grab things. God will bring my own at the right and appropriate time and place.

- if the people I met in a system do not err, and are not under punishment, I should not ordinarily expect to be promoted above them!

(ii) A God-given ability to quietly see every experience (both positive and negative, pleasant and unpleasant), as opportunities and extract needed lessons therefrom. This has helped me a lot - in marriage, workplace, general relationships, and especially in ministry.

Three cases or experiences are worth mentioning here:

(a) In Romans 8:28, we read:

NKJV -

"28 And we know that all things work together for good to those who love God, to those who are the called according to His purpose."

NLT –

"28 And we know that God causes everything to work together for the good of those who love God and are called according to his purpose for them.)

By this verse, I began to see God at work. Rather than bemoan events around me, I started seeing God at work in my life and situations. This has freed me from worries and anxiety. (See also Gen 45:1-8; Phil 4:4-8).

(b) In year 2000 (or thereabouts), as part of the Facilitators in an Orientation/Induction Course for the newly appointed State Pastors, I was asked to speak on "Who Is A State Pastor?" Among other things the Session was used to discuss the importance of- 'faithfulness'. It was emphasised that when a person is faithful, he or she would in fact be building a future for him/herself, as well their children.

As at the writing of this book, - now well over twenty years later, I can see some officers, and Pastors in particular, who through faithfulness, God had lifted up. In the same vein, I could also see several people who are not where they ought to be all because of their unfaithfulness (Luke 16:1-3, 10-13).

(c) Of Schemers and Merchants in the Temple: In Jeremiah 17:9, the Bible emphatically stated that:

"The heart is deceitful above all things, And desperately wicked; Who can know it?"

Whenever I read or hear this Verse I always thought it was talking about the unbelievers or the 'yet-to-be-regenerated' souls. It was when I got to a particular mission field in the course of our ministry work that my eyes 'opened', even as I started to encounter some people who claim to be pastors – spirit-filled, tongue-talking. Their words and actions outside of the pulpit, made the hypocrisy of the Pharisees and Scribes of Jesus' days in Judea, a child's play. They were indeed of desperately wicked hearts – heady, disobedient, self-seeking, and even out to maim and kill anyone who will not let them have their ways!

(iii)   There is no person or situation that is 100% good or bad! Each person or situation may have both (good and bad) in varying proportions.

4.4

PUSHED INTO DESTINY

As I conclude this section of this autobiography, there is an additional voice I will like to talk about. I can call it the *"Second Voice."* Most people have such near or around them.

For Joseph, such a voice came in various forms - as a voice of envy, hatred, and even dream killers through his brothers. The voice also came from Mrs. Potiphar, in the form of lies and eventual imprisonment. Still, for Joseph, the voice came in form of abandonment from those he met and helped (while in the prison), who forgot everything about him for close to two years. In the end, however, all these voices combined to push Joseph to his destiny!

For Samson, the voice was that of an unquenchable desire for a sexual relationship with anything in a skirt! This voice made Samson disobey and probably insulted his very father and mother. This voice eventually landed Samson in the laps of Delilah who succeeded in reducing a strong and highly anointed man of God to a grinder of corn in the enemy's shrine - what a terrible degradation!

 I AM ABRAHAM

Until Samson's life and ministry were prematurely ended, that voice did not let him loose!

In Hannah's case, the voice came from Penninah - the other wife to Hannah's husband. She pestered Hannah's life and made her bitter because she was barren. That voice of the mocker, however, pushed Hannah to a desperate prayer in Shiloh. In the end, Hannah became the mother of five children in addition to Samuel – who unarguably, is one of the greatest of Israel's prophets on an unusual assignment.

For David, the voice came one afternoon and sent him to go and behold a lady who was innocently taking her bath. That voice did not leave David till he sent for the woman, slept with her, and later sent for her husband, Uriah. David made Uriah drunk to lure him to go and sleep with Bathsheba, but the man never did! Finally, David, still under a push by this voice, with his hand wrote a letter master-minding Uriah's murder. This ugly and evil voice was intended to terminate and put a seal on the eternal destiny of David, but God, in His infinite mercy stepped in.

Gehazi heard this second voice in form of greed, covetousness, and lies. It pushed him to run after Naaman - the Assyrian Brigadier-General who had just been miraculously healed of his age-long leprosy. The result was that Gehazi (and his children forever) inherited Naaman's leprosy.

For Saul of Tarsus (who later became the great Apostle Paul), the voice was in form of pride and religion. These pushed him to persecute the first set of early followers of Christ. On a particular trip, that destructive voice was overpowered by the First Voice, and it led to Saul's conversion and commissioning. The transformation that ensued from this encounter was dramatic. Not only did the former persecutor acquire a new nature and destiny, but he also got a new name too. Today, Apostle Paul is renowned for the great exploits he did for God, and also for the unique damages he did to the kingdom of Satan!

Perhaps you too have had a particular voice in your life. This voice may have said (and may even be saying) many things to you. It may have called you various names. At times this voice may have provoked you, made you feel unwanted, of little or no value, and nearly robbed you of self-worth! I have good news for you: The First Voice is superior to whatever any second or even a third voice may be saying (Lamentations 3:37). In the end, it would be obvious that this voice was directly or indirectly pushing you towards your destiny.

Some particular voices have also come my way on many occasions. They combined to invariably push me to God - the only place I could run to for refuge and solace. It was a place of discovery. It was there I found self-worth and genuine peace.

 I AM ABRAHAM

From all the foregoing, I believe it is now obvious that not all *"second voices"* are evil. Some of them may be what God needed you to hear to stir you up unto that which would help your assignment in life. It may be a voice of love that sought to bring the best out of you, even though often coming roughly, aggressively, and perhaps wounding your ego.

A voice came and began to speak loudly to me and around me a little over thirty-six years ago. Specifically on February 1st, 1986. Today, I have every cause to be grateful for that voice. It is the voice behind many revelations I received from God - The First Voice. It is the voice behind many books God has helped me to write. It is the voice behind many major decisions I have taken. That voice has been the voice of my wife – Jane Adesola Haastrup – a wonderfully and fearfully made daughter of Zion.

Jane is a woman of many parts! She is intelligent, hardworking, visionary, agile, and full of energy. In terms of spirituality, she is highly gifted. She is a teacher of the Word, a lady Evangelist, a prayer warrior, and very aggressive against evil, sin, Satan (and all his agents - be they outside or inside the Church), as well as against all compromises.

My wife, Jane, is a deep thinker and a detailed planner. These dual God-given attributes manifest in virtually all she does; when she speaks, prays, praises, and worships God, and of course, when she appreciates you, or you cross her way, and she had cause to rebuke you!

A very important aspect of my wife is her attitude to God and all things pertaining to Him - His Word (particularly His voice to her), His Holy Spirit, His worship, His true servants, His service or call, and sinners - the souls that Jesus, God's own Son – shed His precious blood for.

On several occasions, my wife's faith in God and His Word had made her take some critical or even drastic decisions. These, in the long run, had made her an achiever, as well as a trailblazer - both in her family, among her peers, and even in spiritual matters. For instance, in 1983, against all discouragements, even from Brethren, but based upon God's vivid word to her, she came to the Redeemed Christian Church of God as a Youth Corper and had to become a lecturer at the church's Bible College that just moved to the Redemption Camp (then a jungle in the midst of nowhere), to do the one-year compulsory National Youth Service. To God be all the glory.

Jane is also a very generous giver. Hardly can anybody visit her and leave empty-handed.

On many occasions, God had used her sensitivity to the Holy Spirit to save us as a family from several dangers and catastrophes. Two instances are worth referring to here:

 I AM ABRAHAM

One Sunday morning on Redemption Camp (after we had been posted back to Lagos), we woke up and got ready to go for worship in one of the parishes on the Camp. Suddenly (at least to me), my wife said she wasn't going to church again. Initially, and ordinarily, for someone who normally and usually always got ready far earlier than I do, that decision sounded awkward. All the same, I left, and she remained in the house. While the service was going on, a lady came to call me that a thief had broken into our house - through the ceiling. At that time, thieves used to break into houses when most, if not all Camp residents went to Church. On this historic day, hearing the noise of all the intruder was doing in trying to break the ceiling so as to force his way into the main sitting room, my wife managed to run out of the house. She raised an alarm and called the attention of the brethren passing by. To the glory of God, the thief was apprehended, beaten, and handed over to Camp security personnel. How great is our God!

According to Jane, one of the things she was taught very early in her Christian life is the discipline of hearing God's voice. The moment she is fully convinced of the Lord's voice, nothing - whether men, friends, foes, colleagues, subordinates or even leaders could make her act against that *"First Voice!"*

On another occasion, while on pilgrimage to the Holy land (Israel), we were preparing to go for the evening meal. It was a day when we had had a long trip to many places, and everybody was tired and greatly hungry! Then, God spoke to Jane not to go and have her dinner. She was to remain in God's presence - praying in the Spirit. I left her in the room and on my way, I met someone who had been sent to come and lead us to a place where the table had been set. We were being expected to join some very senior pastors in a sumptuous buffet dinner. To the glory of God, Jane politely explained the clear instructions God had given her, and stood her ground!

Let me give one more testimony of the determined mind that God has given her. When it comes to waiting on the Lord in prayers with fasting, she could go 30-40 days more than once or twice in a single year!

A multi-talented, multi-tasked, highly spiritual woman of God, and the mother of our two lovely children, may the Lord continue to be Jane's unfailing strength in Jesus' Name, Amen.

Over the years, God has taught me not to take her for granted - even if I don't agree with or cannot readily discern the basis for what she said. I pray that God will uphold her to the very end and that we, with all our children and their own seeds too, will make it home to Heaven in the end. To God be all the glory.

Abraham - in His Room at the University of Birmingham, UK, 1990

Abraham and Fellowship Brethren at Birmingham, UK 1990

Abraham in Melbourne (2021)

Jane in Melbourne (2021)

Abraham & Jane in Melbourne (2021)

Pst Abraham Haastrup With Daddy GO and other Members of RCCG Governing Council (Lagos, August 2018).

Pst Abraham Haastrup With Daddy GO (Lagos, 2018).

4.5

LIVING TESTIMONIES

As said earlier in this autobiography, God brought me into this world on Friday, 11th January 1952. I thank God that I am still alive and well. I praise Him too that I am not insane, and I am not in an asylum. In addition, I am grateful to God that I am not in the grave (Psalm 89:1, Dan 6:1-4, 21-21, Isaiah 43:2). Finally, I thank God that in His mercy He saved my soul and also kept me alive.

The purpose of this chapter is to recall some of the several things that had happened both before and ever since I got saved that could ordinarily have terminated my life. I will just mention a few of them that are so vivid. Whenever I recount them, I still marvel at the mercy and sovereignty of God:

Ijebu Igbo (South-West, Nigeria) -1967

An electrician came into our premises to fix the fluorescents in the compound. Innocently I decided to offer him (an Igbo guy) some assistance. So, I climbed the drum he was standing on. Looking down about a minute or two later, I saw a snake right where I was standing just before. I didn't know where it came from. I raised an alarm and the man jumped down, pursued, and killed the snake.

Birmingham (West-Midlands, United Kingdom) - December 1989

I went to worship in one church and met a Christian brother - a Nigerian. After service, he followed me to my University hostel. In return, the following Wednesday, I too decided to visit him at the address he gave me - it was at a high-rise estate. I think I mistook the Block and Flat He gave me (Block 14/7 or Block 7/14). I got there and knocked, and a white man welcomed me in with a smile. I told him who I was looking for, and that I may have missed my way. He said there was no problem. As I proceeded to the door, he asked where I was going. He asked if I had any money on me, and I said yes. He demanded all the money. I told him that I am a student. Then he brought out a knife! It was then I knew that I was in serious trouble. Up till now, I didn't know where the boldness came from, I told him I can't give him my money. So I went towards the door, he already bolted it. One way or the other, I escaped unhurt!

Oshogbo (South-West, Nigeria) - 1999)

Around midnight, we heard a scream from a couple living directly under our flat. We were on the 2nd floor of the 2storey 4-Flat house. My wife said we should go down and see if we could be of help. So, we ran downstairs. We didn't know they were being attacked by two young boys who were armed robbers. To cut a long story short, they welcomed us and were bold enough to say they were visitors to the couple. So, we turned to go, but they halted us! They followed us to our flat at gunpoint, ransacked our house, made away with a cash sum of N59,000.00, our international passports, and some other items. They locked us up in the toilet and went with the key! Somehow, we were able to open the door. We thank God that He did not let them harm us. The cash they took away was the school fees of my niece - a medical student who was staying with us.

Deliverances from motor Accidents (Between 2000 and 2003):

More than twice, God supernaturally delivered us from accidents on Lagos-Ibadan expressway. On one occasion, the driver slept off on the wheel and veered off going in between the two sides of the roads. On another occasion, I believe God spoke to the driver to leave a particular lane. Almost as soon as he did, we just began to hear "Gba!", "Gba!" A petrol tanker truck had lost control and was just clearing all the vehicles in its way. Several deaths were recorded on that day. (The incident happened near the Redemption Camp).

Dallas, Texas, USA (June 2010)

We had just finished the RCCGNA Convention. I was going to the airport for a connecting flight (Dallas-Washington-Addis Ababa). The brother driving us slept off and veered to the other side facing oncoming vehicles. It must have been the Holy Spirit that woke me and Pastor Bamidele Sturdivant up. Thank God no vehicle was on coming. It was a mighty deliverance. The car was heading towards a vast Lake on the other side of the road!

In addition to all these instances enumerated, there were several nights that I went to bed, without much assurance of waking up the following mornings. I can go on and on. But in all these things, God has made us more than conquerors! (Psalm 89:1, 22-24, Romans 8:31). To Him alone be ALL the glory and praise!

4.6

ONCE, I WAS YOUNG

"I have been young, and now am old; Yet I have not seen the righteous forsaken, Nor his descendants begging bread." (Psalm 37:25)

The above text was credited to the man David – obviously one of the greatest men who ever lived in history. For our purpose here, we will look at three things in the verse:

- I have been young;
- And now I am old; and
- Yet I have not seen the righteous forsaken, Nor his descendants begging bread.

I have been young (or I was once a young man): Among other things, I believe David is saying here:

I was once young! Once, David was like an average youth of today. He was in their shoes - He was their age. He understood what they are going through. Maybe you are a youth reading this book. Once, David was like you! He

was in your shoes - He was your age. He understood what you are going through – the peer pressures, the frustration you have, especially thinking that your parents can't see from your worldview. The emotional trauma you are experiencing – of the inner urges to experiment with drugs, sex, and so on. David had the opportunity to think the way you are thinking now, and even to act the way you are acting now. He seems to be saying to you: *"I could have loved what you are loving now. I could have dressed the way some of you are dressing now."* He seems to be saying further: *"But I did not! Why didn't I? Or, why couldn't I? Because something within me kept on telling me, "You are different", "God has a great plan for you"; "You are a child of destiny!"*

(b) Once, I was young! No matter when and where you are born, you can only be young once in a lifetime! You cannot be young twice. Thus, if you miss it or you waste your youth, you can never recover it! What is this telling us? The choice you make in your youth is going to determine who and what you become in life. The time of youth is a foundation stage. Psalm 11:3 says:

"If the foundations are destroyed, What can the righteous do?"

This clearly means that if your foundation is wrong or its faulty, there is no prayer and fasting that can change it. If anything will ever change for the better, it will be by the special Divine intervention and sovereignty of God!

Now I am old: What is David saying here?

(a) Watch what you do and the way you do things as a youth, because whether you believe it or not, very soon, you will be like me now! Hence, live right and be an agent of transformation - maximize your life for God. Be the salt of the earth and the light of the world. Add value to others (Ecclesiastes 12:1-7, John 9:4-5).

(b) Now, I am old - All the things I sowed in my youth are what I am reaping now (both good and bad - 1 Samuel 16:18). My faithfulness, my investment in others, my strength and gallantry, my once-in-a-lifetime carelessness and infidelity with Bathsheba – the wife of Uriah, my loyal soldier, etc, I cannot reverse anything now! (1 Timothy 4:16).

I have never seen the righteous forsaken, nor his seed beg for bread: Again, David is trying to tell us here that:

(a) If there is anything I did wrong, and I am suffering for, or regretting today, God is not to be blamed, I am the one to blame! Why? Because God is righteous (Acts 10:34-35, Psalm 112:1-3, Psalm 128:1-6). So, take heed. Live right today, and you will never regret it tomorrow!

(b) Matthew 6:33 - Have the right priority. Just do the

 I AM ABRAHAM

will of God in your generation, and surely God will take care of your seed and future.

The things some of our parents had were the best the technology of their generation could give - houses, cars, etc. Some of our parents got those things with the hope that they would make life easier for us. Today, those things are obsolete and many of us cannot use them. Some of us are even far from home, and those things are not relevant to us or useful for us.

Maybe you have not been saved (Romans 3:23; 6:23, Acts 4:12, 1 John 1:5-9, Isaiah 55:6-7, Proverbs 28:13, Romans 10:9-13).

Maybe God opened the door for you to come to where you are. What have you been doing with your life? Has coming to such a land of unlimited opportunities become a license to a loose life? Are you like that prodigal son who took all he had and went to a country far away to waste his life and resources? One day like today, that prodigal son came to his senses and said, *"What am I doing here! I will arise and go back to my father's house."* Today, God is calling you to your senses. He is saying to you, arise, come back home!

That age-long Hymn, says:

"Just as I am, without one plea

But that Thy blood was shed for me And that Thou bid'st me come to Thee

O Lamb of God, I come! I come..."

It's time to pray:

- Father, thank You for Your Word to me and for me. Please give a new beginning today.

- Everywhere I have taken Your goodness for granted, Father, please forgive me.

- Father, anything I will do in my youth that will bring me sorrow in my old age, please don't let me do it.

- Father, please help me to maximize my days as a youth for Your glory.

You may have read this Book so far, and you are an adult – perhaps in the second half of life (above 50 years old). Have you looked back to your past and some sense of regret or nostalgia overwhelmed you? May be you are already asking "Is there anything I can do?" or "Where do I begin?" Yes, you can begin by crying to God – Your Creator and Maker. You can ask Him for mercy. You can ask Him to restore your wasted years, and give you another chance

– a brand new beginning:

"*15 For He says to Moses, "I will have mercy on whomever I will have mercy, and I will have compassion on whomever I will have compassion." 16 So then it is not of him who wills, nor of him who runs, but of God who shows mercy."…. "18 Do not remember the former things, Nor consider the things of old. 19 Behold, I will do a new thing, Now it shall spring forth; Shall you not know it? I will even make a road in the wilderness And rivers in the desert."…. "12 Now, therefore," says the Lord, "Turn to Me with all your heart, With fasting, with weeping, and with mourning." 13 So rend your heart, and not your garments; Return to the Lord your God, For He is gracious and merciful, Slow to anger, and of great kindness; And He relents from doing harm. 14 Who knows if He will turn and relent, And leave a blessing behind Him — A grain offering and a drink +offering For the Lord your God?....*

24 The threshing floors shall be full of wheat, And the vats shall overflow with new wine and oil. 25 "So I will restore to you the years that the swarming locust has eaten, The crawling locust, The consuming locust, And the chewing locust, My great army which I sent among you. 26 You shall eat in plenty and be satisfied, And praise the name of the Lord your God, Who has dealt wondrously with you; And My people shall never be put to shame. 27 Then you shall know that I am in the midst of Israel: I am the Lord your God And there is no other. My people shall never be put to shame." - Romans 9:15-16; Isa 43:18-19; Joel 2:12-14, 24-27.

Jane with her heart-throb Abraham's 70th Birthday

Abraham towards 70th Birthday

Abraham & Jane towards Abraham's 70th Birthday.

Abraham & Jane's love never dies

 I AM ABRAHAM

Abraham & Jane in Melbourne (Nov, 2021)

*Abraham & Jane at 70th Birthday Reception,
Melbourne - Australia (8th Jan, 2022).*

PART 5

TO WHOM MUCH IS GIVEN

- **5.1** TO WHOM MUCH IS GIVEN
- **5.2** POSSESSING YOUR POSSESSION
- **5.3** LONGING FOR THE EVENING!
- **5.4** APPROACHING GOD'S PRESENCE
- **5.5** SPIRITUAL READING OF THE WORD

5.1

TO WHOM MUCH IS GIVEN

There are many things that God has graciously given us as human beings and in particular, those of us who, in His mercy, had been redeemed by the Blood of Jesus – our Saviour, Lord, and King. The truth is that God who had given us so much, also has some expectations- He expects us to be faithful stewards of His manifold graces (1 Corinthians 4:2; Luke 16:1-3, 10-12). May God help us to be faithful in Jesus' name.

One of the things that vividly dawned on me a decade ago, when I turned sixty, was the fact that God in His mercy had been extraordinarily good and gracious to me as an individual. If Jesus had not saved me when He did (on that Wednesday 8th of July 1981), all things put together, I might not have reached the age of sixty then, not to talk of being alive to now clock seventy! I thank God that the multitude of His mercy had seen me through this far, and also thus far (1 Sam. 7:12).

In Romans 12:1-2(NLT), we read:

"And so, dear brothers and sisters, I plead with you to give your bodies to God because of all he has done for you. Let them be a living and holy sacrifice—the kind he will find acceptable. This is truly the way to worship him. Don't copy the behavior and customs of this world, but let God transform you into a new person by changing the way you think. Then you will learn to know God's will for you, which is good and pleasing and perfect."

It is this Scripture that made me resolve to stick more to God's standards rather than conform to the ever-shifting world, cultural or even organizational standards.

In Luke 12:48b, we read:

"But he who did not know, yet committed things deserving of stripes, shall be beaten with few. For everyone to whom much is given, from him much will be required; and to whom much has been committed, of him they will ask the more."

Hence, I also began to ask God to continue to show me what He expected of me - His good, acceptable, and perfect will. One of the ways God has been answering these prayers is that He began to help me to know the difference between God's will and God's mind. The Bible, in many places, clearly states the will of God - what God wants and expects would be done in the ultimate. For example, it is the will of God that all men be saved. He even made provisions for the salvation of all men (Ezekiel 18:23, Romans 5:6-8, John 3:16-18, Acts 4:12, Romans 10:9-13, 1 John 1:7-9, etc).

However, in Acts 16:6-10, the Holy Spirit prevented Paul and his team from embarking on two trips to go and preach. On arrival at a place, Apostle Paul had a vision and saw a man beckoning and saying to him, "Come over to Macedonia." They took it as a sign that it was where God wanted them to go for that particular moment. Thus, while the Bible declares the will of God, it takes the Holy Spirit to reveal or make clear the mind of God. 1 Corinthians 2:9-12 (NLT) says:

"That is what the Scriptures mean when they say, "No eye has seen, no ear has heard, and no mind has imagined what God has prepared for those who love him." But it was to us that God revealed these things by his Spirit. For his Spirit searches out everything and shows us God's deep secrets. No one can know a person's thoughts except that person's own spirit, and no one can know God's thoughts except God's own Spirit. And we have received God's Spirit (not the world's spirit), so we can know the wonderful things God has freely given us."

The mind of God has to do with the how, where, and when His stated will is to be done. When we are genuinely saved and filled with the Holy Spirit, the mind of God starts to be clear to us. The question then is, how do we receive the mind of God, and ensure that the mind of God overrides our human mind and spirit? This can only happen when we have stayed in His presence when we have spent quality time with Him through His Word, and prayer. The Word of God has the power to sanctify us. The Word takes away all fleshly desires or imaginations that can deafen our ears or distort what God may be saying to us:

"16 All Scripture is inspired by God and is useful to teach us what is true and to make us realize what is wrong in our lives. It corrects us when we are wrong and teaches us to do what is right. 17 God uses it to prepare and equip his people to do every good work." 2 Timothy 3:16-17 (NLT)

"17Sanctify them by Your truth. Your word is truth. 18As You sent Me into the world, I also have sent them into the world. 19And for their sakes I sanctify Myself, that they also may be sanctified by the truth." John 17:17-19 (NLT)

"1And so, dear brothers and sisters, I plead with you to give your bodies to God because of all he has done for you. Let them be a living and holy sacrifice—the kind he will find acceptable. This is truly the way to worship him. 2Don't copy the behavior and customs of this world, but let God transform you into a new person by changing the way you think. Then you will learn to know God's will for you, which is good and pleasing and perfect." Romans 12:1-2 (NLT) (See also Hebrews 4:12)

 I AM ABRAHAM

As we pray too, God begins to impress upon our mind what He wants us to do. Still talking about Luke 12:48, our Lord Jesus said,

"But he who did not know, yet committed things deserving of stripes, shall be beaten with few. For everyone to whom much is given, from him much will be required; and to whom much has been committed, of him they will ask the more."

Often in life, many people don't ask God what He expects from them in return for all He has done for them, and for the vast opportunities He had given them, or for all the great doors He has opened for them. Having acknowledged that God had given me so much in life, as I continued to pray, the word *"influence"* – a positive global influence – began to take root in my mind.

Esther – a young female orphan whom God raised through her uncle, Mordecai – nearly fell into that same error too. In a foreign land, God's favor located her, and she became the Queen to, perhaps the most powerful king on earth then. Thank God that Mordecai knew why God had done so much for the young lady. He, Mordecai, emphatically alerted and told Esther the reasons:

"Mordecai sent this reply to Esther: "Don't think for a moment that because you're in the palace you will escape when all other Jews are killed. If you keep quiet at a time like this, deliverance and relief for the Jews will arise from some other place, but you

and your relatives will die. Who knows if perhaps you were made queen for just such a time as this?" Esther 4:13-14 (NLT).

Queen Esther realized this truth, and immediately did what God expected of her:

"Then Esther sent this reply to Mordecai: "Go and gather together all the Jews of Susa and fast for me. Do not eat or drink for three days, night or day. My maids and I will do the same. And then, though it is against the law, I will go in to see the king. If I must die, I must die." Esther 4:15-16.

At times, we need some spiritually discerning people around us to help jolt us into knowing and doing the right things when the need arises. God had put such people in my life on several occasions. For instance, in 1990, on returning from the United Kingdom where it became clear that God was calling me into full-time ministry, I made up my mind and was prepared to resign from my appointment with the Lagos State Government (as an Administrative Officer). I just felt led to go and share my plans with an elderly Christian and also a senior officer in government (Rev John Dansu). After hearing the testimony of my conviction about the call, he asked how many years I still had in the State Service before I would be qualified for voluntary retirement. I told him it remained about twelve to fifteen months. He counseled that I should prayerfully consider waiting till then, and leave on a clean note. After due consideration, I thank God that He helped me to agree to that fatherly advice. It was much later I realized the several unpleasant implications my leaving earlier would have had if I had left as I intended on my own. Two of these consequences were that I would have been asked to refund all the salaries paid to me while on the oversee program. Also, I might have blocked the chances of other Christians, as my action would have created a wrong impression that any Christian sent abroad could bolt away under the cover of "a Call of God" Rather than all these, my waiting and clean break from Public Service led to an official release and commendation, as well as an elaborate send-forth ceremony. Every time I remember this critical time in my life, I always thank God for sending such a man of God my way.

In my over thirty years of full-time Christian service in the RCCG, God has taught me many things - about life, ministry, leadership, and human beings. That God made me survive many things and also saw me through the hierarchies to the level of an AGO (Assistant General Overseer), as well as to the position of a Continental Overseer were nothing but the mighty hand of our great God. Even in all these, I realize it was for a purpose, and that purpose is His Kingdom. Standing before King Agrippa, Apostle Paul testified:

"[21]Some Jews arrested me in the Temple for preaching this, and

they tried to kill me. ²²But God has protected me right up to this present time so I can testify to everyone, from the least to the greatest. I teach nothing except what the prophets and Moses said would happen -" Acts 26:21-22 (NLT)

In conclusion, in Genesis 32:10, the man Jacob said: *"I am not worthy of all the unfailing love and faithfulness you have shown to me, your servant. When I left home and crossed the Jordan River, I owned nothing except a walking stick. Now my household fills two large camps!"* (Emphasis Added)

The words *"When I left home"* in the above text caught my attention. In my 70 Years of life, I have had to leave many homes. Yet, I perceive there are still two *"homes"* ahead! - one more to leave, and one yet to be entered.

The home to leave is this world. If one is not careful, it is so easy to think this world is a home to be, and you can begin to put all you are, and all you have into it. In Matthew 6:19-21, our Lord told us:

"¹⁹Don't store up treasures here on earth, where moths eat them and rust destroys them, and where thieves break in and steal. ²⁰ Store your treasures in heaven, where moths and rust cannot destroy, and thieves do not break in and steal. ²¹ Wherever your treasure is, there the desires of your heart will also be."

Dear reader, the world has become too old or very aged for you to think it is the best place to invest your life and all.

 I AM ABRAHAM

Not only did our Lord Jesus assure us of a far better place, (as in the above passage), He and Apostle Peter told us what would become of this world as we now know it:

"9 The Lord isn't really being slow about his promise, as some people think. No, he is being patient for your sake. He does not want anyone to be destroyed, but wants everyone to repent. 10 But the day of the Lord will come as unexpectedly as a thief. Then the heavens will pass away with a terrible noise, and the very elements themselves will disappear in fire, and the earth and everything on it will be found to deserve judgment. 11 Since everything around us is going to be destroyed like this, what holy and godly lives you should live, 12 looking forward to the day of God and hurrying it along. On that day, he will set the heavens on fire, and the elements will melt away in the flames." 2 Peter 3:9-12 (NLT) (See also Matt 24:1-3; John 14:1-3)

There is a home to enter. That home is Heaven. Heaven is not an imaginary place. It is real. That is where God wants all His children to be with Him forever (John 14:1-6, Revelations 21:1-7). Will you love to be there, to live there forever? If yes, the time to start preparing is NOW!

"Seek the Lord while He may be found, Call upon Him while He is near. 7 Let the wicked forsake his way, And the unrighteous man his thoughts; Let him return to the Lord, And He will have mercy on him; And to our God, For He will abundantly pardon.... "13He who covers his sins will not prosper, But

whoever confesses and forsakes them will have mercy."

(Isaiah 55:6-7, Proverbs 38:13 (See also Revelation 21:8, Hebrews 12:14).

May God see us through, in Jesus' name. Amen.

5.2

POSSESSING YOUR POSSESSION

" ¹When Abram was ninety-nine years old, the Lord appeared to Abram and said to him, "I am Almighty God; walk before Me and be blameless. ²And I will make My covenant between Me and you, and will multiply you exceedingly." ³Then Abram fell on his face, and God talked with him, saying: ⁴"As for Me, behold, My covenant is with you, and you shall be a father of many nations. ⁵No longer shall your name be called Abram, but your name shall be Abraham; for I have made you a father of many nations. ⁶I will make you exceedingly fruitful; and I will make nations of you, and kings shall come from you. ⁷And I will establish My covenant between Me and you and your descendants after you in their generations, for an everlasting covenant, to be God to you and your descendants after you. ⁸Also I give to you and your descendants after you the land in which you are a stranger, all the land of Canaan, as an everlasting possession; and I will be their God." ⁹And God said to Abraham: "As for you, you shall keep My covenant, you and your descendants after you throughout their generations." Genesis 17:1-9

" ³*May God Almighty bless you and give you many children. And may your descendants multiply and become many nations!* ⁴*May God pass on to you and your descendants the blessings he promised to Abraham. May you own this land where you are now living as a foreigner, for God gave this land to Abraham.*" Genesis 28:3-4 (NLT).

In this chapter, we shall be looking at our subject from 3 perspectives:

- First, the Word Possession - what does it mean?

- Second, how do we possess our possession? Can we do it on our own, or do we need some assistance in doing so? If yes, who then can help us possess our possession?

- Third, some action steps that we need to take to possess our possession

Before going into the details on all the above three perspectives, it is very crucial to point out that as a Covenant keeping God, He demands that for each generation to continue to enjoy the blessings of a covenant entered into with their fathers, they must determinedly obey the terms of the Covenant. In our text above, God told Abraham: "your responsibility is to obey the terms of the Covenant. You and all your descendants have this continual responsibility." "Any male who fails to be

circumcised will be cut off from the Covenant family for breaking the Covenant" (Gen. 17:9, 13-14).

The word Possession has many connotations. Among others, it means;

- the act of taking control - whether legally or without permission

- domination

- the crime of having something illegal (such as drugs or weapons).

The one definition or use that is relevant to our discussion here is the one that describes possession as:

- ownership of something, or as something that is owned or possessed by someone.

* It can be a tangible or physical thing - (for example a landed property). It may also be something intangible or spiritual.

* A possession can be territorial or generational.

* Some possessions are passed on to us by our parents for example, Naboth's Vineyard - I Kings 21:1-20. Also, the Prodigal son and his brother - Luke 15:11-32).

* Some possessions are divinely allocated to us by God

(for example, in our text, God told Abraham, *"the land in which you are now a stranger, I have given unto you and your seed or descendants forever (as an everlasting possession)"* - a heritage.

* Of course, there are some possessions we acquire or accumulate over years as a result of hard work, diligence, faithfulness, right living, and investments.

There are some things to note when we talk about possessions:

- we have to know what has been allocated to us as a possession.

- It is also our responsibility to possess and defend it.

- More than all these, we must add value to our possession - both for our benefit, and for the sake of posterity.

- An important fact that many people often ignore, when it comes to the subject of possessing our possession, is that there is an adversary who is all out to hinder us from, or rob us of our possession. He can use anything and anyone. (1 Peter 5:8-9, 2 Corinthians 10:3-6, Ephesians 6:10-18).

 I AM ABRAHAM

How do We Possess Our Possession?

The first step in possessing our possession is knowledge. It is impossible to possess what you don't even know exists or had been given to you. So, we need knowledge - the knowledge that there is an allocated possession for you. Still talking about knowledge, we must discover and locate our possession - we need to know the extent, the dimensions, the boundaries or perimeter (length, breadth, height, and depth of it). It is this knowledge (of the dimensions) that will help us know the state of our possession - for example, are there any illegal occupants, trespassers or defilers, etc., on the possession?

A man had large hectares of land somewhere. He left it for long. He did not cultivate it, he never bothered to fence it up. Years went by. Then one day, he woke up and visited the land. He was shocked by what he found. Some parts had been dug and the earth carried away to go and fill up some places, another part already had a building foundation. He also discovered that the river that passed through the rear part of his land had become a fish pond that somebody had been making money from! - several illegal occupants, intruders, trespassers! Many of us are ignorant of what God has allocated to us, and several illegal occupants, intruders, trespassers are feeding fat on what belongs to us.

The question then arises, can we possess our possessions all by ourselves? Often, the answer is No! Why? It is because the illegal occupants, the intruders, the trespassers are not easy to dislodge - they are daredevils. They are prepared to do anything to stay put on what is not theirs. Hence, we must be ready to contend with them and claim our heritage, we must prepare to take some steps, dislodge them, and also do some things to forbid further advancement of these adversaries.

This is where we need divine assistance. The only One who can help us possess our possession is God. The Bible described Him as Jehovah, the Man of War (one Version called Him *"The LORD OF HEAVEN'S ARMIES"*) In Psalm 24:7-10, we read:

"⁷Lift up your heads, O you gates! And be lifted up, you everlasting doors! And the King of glory shall come in. ⁸Who is this King of glory? The Lord strong and mighty, The Lord mighty in battle. ⁹Lift up your heads, O you gates! Lift up, you everlasting doors! And the King of glory shall come in. ¹⁰Who is this King of glory? The Lord of hosts, He is the King of glory."

As you are reading this book, I want to suggest some practical actions to you:

- Take a pen, list out what you consider as your possessions - physically (your health, your wealth, your career, your marriage, and family), spiritually (your salvation, sanctification, fruit, and gifts of the Holy Spirit, God's presence in your life, Heaven), etc.

- What is their current state or value? Are there any intruders or trespassers? Deal with them one by one. If you have now come to realize that some things are not what they ought to be, then you know you need help - you need Divine Assistance. Thank God for the Man of war, the Lord of Heaven's Armies, the unseen force that can handle your seen and unseen enemies and trespassers.

In addition to the foregoing, there are more actions you must take:

- You must add value to your possession - invest it, or invest in it.

- You must make God your senior partner. It is one thing for God to help you possess or recover your possession, it is another thing for you to continue to retain it. (Exodus Chapters 12-14). For permanent security, preservation, and enhanced value of your possession, you need to make God the CEO of your possession.

- You must speak to some strategic points in your possessions and possess them. I call them GATES (Psalm 24:7-10). The enemy will want to use these gates to intrude and re-enter your possession.

As we conclude, let me add the following:

- The I AM is the One who gives possession, He can also drive out and dispossess somebody of his/her possession if the one given the possession does not value or add value to the possession (like Esau). What is this telling us? Don't joke with your possession! Value it, contend for it, and add value to it. Don't hide it from your children. Rather, from time to time, show it to them and ask them too to value it, contend for it, and add value to it!

Genesis 28:12-13:

"Then he dreamed, and behold, a ladder was set up on the earth, and its top reached to heaven; and there the angels of God were ascending and descending on it. And behold, the Lord stood above it and said: "I am the Lord God of Abraham your father and the God of Isaac; the land on which you lie I will give to you and your descendants."

It's time to pray. I believe the following prayer points will surely help you:

- Father, thank You for this special day of truth and discovery. Thank You for all you have divinely allocated to me.

 I AM ABRAHAM

- Father, please forgive me of any evil complacency. Forgive me for any alliance or cooperation with those who are my adversaries.

- Open my eyes to see, to discover, recover and possess my possession (Psalm 144:1; Isaiah 49:24-26). Father, please teach my hands to war, and my fingers to fight!

- Every trespasser on my possession - sickness, demons, Satan, ancestral, territorial spirits - I serve you quit notice. I forbid your further advancements.

- I declare and make all God has given unto me a 'NO GO' area for you Satan, demons, ancestral spirits, etc. in the Mighty Name of Jesus.

- Lord, I make you my Senior Partner, take over and secure me and all my possession - life, family, children, career, etc.

- I discover, recover and possess my possession in Jesus' name.

Are you living as a stranger in the land that God has given to you? Or, you have already sold your birthright to the Canaanites, and they are bastardizing and defiling what God gave you. You are going to tell them that ENOUGH IS ENOUGH!

Final Action!

Are you living in sin, or you are following bad/evil people? If yes, you are at great risk! This is because in that state you cannot discover, not to talk of possessing your possessions. As we have already seen, it is God who can help you. If you are not on the side of God, your future and destiny is very bleak and uncertain. But when you give your life to Christ and you begin to follow His ways, then victory is sure for you, and your tomorrow will be alright (Isaiah 3:10-11).

5.3

LONGING FOR THE EVENING!

"My mind reels and my heart races. I longed for evening to come, but now I am terrified of the dark." Isaiah 21:4 (NLT)

As the years rolled by, many things we long for in life may or may not have become a reality.

"To long for something", is to desire and pursue it. What is being longed for could be an improved state or situation. It could also be a place, a person, a season, a change, a position, etc. When a man longs for something, it may turn out to become a passion or pursuit.

Many a time, when what we had longed for eventually comes, they hardly bring lasting satisfaction and fulfillment! This is a part of the stark realities of life. When young, many of us longed to grow up, acquire higher education, get a good job, marry, settle down, build our own house, and if spiritual, go into ministry and make an impact for God's Kingdom (and probably make a name for ourselves). What probably pushed us forward to a new level of pursuit, after every level of achievement or success, was the realization that that level was not satisfying.

Thus (in our text), the Prophet Isaiah longed for the evening. However, when the evening later came, He said he was terrified of the dark. What could be the reason(s). Also, what could have terrified him about the evening and its darkness? First, there are many things "evening" stands for. Evenings are characterized by "darkness" - loneliness, waning strength, low performances, or even losses of vital organs of the body (internal and external) like our brains, eyes, ears, teeth, etc. The loneliness of evenings also helps to cast the mind back and we begin to recall some lost opportunities, people who came our way. Some people may have helped us, many may have betrayed us, denied us, or even injured us. People like the brothers of Joseph, Mrs. Potiphar, the Ahitophels, the Sanballats and Tobiahs, some Simons the Sorcerer, etc. Yet in all these things, we should have a good cause to be grateful to God. This is because one way or the other, God did not let the enemies have an upper hand (Psalm 89:1, 22-24, Romans 8:28).

The best way to prepare and avoid being terrified when the evening comes is to maximize our days – pleasing God, and doing what is right. If and through the help of God (His Word and His Holy Spirit), we can do so, then when the evening comes, we would never be terrified by its darkness. Men and women across the Bible – people like

 I Am Abraham

Abraham, Joseph, Moses, Samuel, David, Elijah, Elisha, the elderly Simeon and Anna, Paul (the Apostle), etc, did so. All these people longed for the evening, and when it came, they rejoiced greatly. They were never terrified! (1 Samuel 12:1-5, Romans 4:21; 2 Timothy 4:6-8).

Whether the evening of a day, the evening of a career, and especially the evening of life, another peculiarity of evenings is that it provides us with a great opportunity to look back to the mornings, and be grateful to God. This is a season to acknowledge His faithfulness - recalling all He had seen or brought us through:

"It is good to give thanks to the Lord, And to sing praises to Your name, O Most High; [2] To declare Your lovingkindness in the morning, And Your faithfulness every night," (Psalm 92:1-2).

By God's grace, as a person, I too have some things I long for in life. I classify them into four:

- Knowing and fulfilling God's purpose.

- Establishing and expanding God's Kingdom and rule in my life, domain, and in my generation.

- Being a carrier of God's presence.

- Reigning with Christ eternally.

Also inherent in all these are what I long for in a marriage and the home.

Concerning The Redeemed Christian Church of God (RCCG) – the Church Denomination that God in His supernatural arrangement connected me with very early in my Christian journey – I have a longing too. There is nothing that I so much cherished, prayed for, did all within my power, and looked forward to, than that God's Kingdom values – righteousness, truth, and justice, etc., be entrenched. I sincerely longed for what I tag "A Psalm 101" organization. In addition, I long for Phase 3 of the Church - A Church prepared and ready for the second coming of the Lord Jesus.

In truth, when you long for something, you must also do some things that will hasten getting what you long for. In my particular case, to know and fulfill God's purpose, with God's help, I decided to, among other things:

• Prioritize the studying of God's WORD (the Holy Bible) to know God intimately, and also discover His Redemptive purpose and plans for me as a person. For some time now, I have kept a daily journal of God's dealings. I have let His Word daily shape my heart, my day, my life, and my destiny.

• God has helped me to daily worship Him, and acknowledge His love, and sovereignty (Psalm 89:1, 22-24,

Numbers 23:19, Romans 8:28).

- God has helped me to rightly position myself (through obedience), where God could easily reach me for direction, assistance and blessings.

- God has helped me to associate myself with like-minded individuals. (Psalm 119:63, 74, 79; 2 Tim. 2:22).

God has helped me to establish and expand His Kingdom, and rule in my life, my domain, and generation. Part of my decision is that with God's help, I would:

- Live right and be a living witness.

- Daily witness, personally lead people to Christ and also prayerfully disciple them.

In addition, God has helped me to be a carrier of His presence. Having discovered the great and utmost importance of God's presence, I asked God to help me to be conscious of the importance of His presence - that it is Heaven to me (Genesis 39:1-23). God has helped me to do all to keep His presence with me, hence I daily pray against, and avoid anything or anyone who is out to take God's presence from me, or to take me from God's presence (whatever, whoever and wherever that thing or person might be - whether a friend or a foe, whether provocations, accusers, flatterers, or obstructers!) - Psalm 1:1-3, John 8:29, 1 Corinthians 9:24-27.

God has helped me to identify the most critical need of our world today - the Gospel (John 8:32, 36, Acts 4:12, Romans 1:16, Psalm 119:105, 130). He is also daily giving me strategies to reach the world for Him through writings – Preaching, Teaching, Tracts, articles, books, social media, networking, etc.

The final thing I long for is to reign with Him. To qualify to reign with Christ eternally, I started listing out (from the Scriptures):

- The things that will qualify me to enter Heaven – living a holy and righteous life (Hebrews 14:12, 1 Corinthians 9:24-27).

- Diligently watching unto the second coming of the Lord (2 Peter 3:7-12).

- Staying away from people and things that easily corrupt, especially in this era of unbridled and uncontrolled internet and social media.

5.4

APPROACHING GOD'S PRESENCE

"Who may worship in your sanctuary, LORD? Who may enter your presence on your holy hill? ² Those who lead blameless lives and do what is right, speaking the truth from sincere hearts. ³ Those who refuse to gossip or harm their neighbors or speak evil of their friends. ⁴ Those who despise flagrant sinners and honor the faithful followers of the LORD, and keep their promises even when it hurts. ⁵ Those who lend money without charging interest, and who cannot be bribed to lie about the innocent. Such people will stand firm forever." Psalm 15:1-5 (NLT)

Our God has several attributes. He is loving, merciful, kind, and faithful. He is also the Almighty, All-seeing, and All-knowing. However, what stands Him out, and what He wants to be known for, above all other things, is His Holiness - our God is HOLY. We can safely say that Holiness is His Trade Mark (and that Trade Mark is patented)!

Whenever we are approaching God's presence, let us keep in mind that we are approaching a HOLY GOD. One can also say that this Holiness has two dimensions - an offensive dimension and a defensive dimension.

Offensive - Holiness offends those who are living in sin. It exposes and accuses them. Holiness also launches war on those who attack the holy (Daniel 6:1-4, 6-24).

Defensive - Holiness defends the holy one. It protects them and makes them untouchable. Holiness also fights for the holy one. For example, in the lions' den, Daniel could not be touched because God sent His angel to shut the mouth of the hungry lions. However, when the accusers of Daniel and all their family members were thrown into the den, the lions had a mastery of them. They did an extra job in eating them up!

In Isaiah 29:13-14 (NLT), we read:

"And so the Lord says, "These people say they are mine. They honor me with their lips, but their hearts are far from me. And their worship of me is nothing but man-made rules learned by rote. Because of this, I will once again astound these hypocrites with amazing wonders. The wisdom of the wise will pass away, and the intelligence of the intelligent will disappear."

In the above Scripture, God accused the Israelites (His people):

"And their worship of me is nothing but man-made rules learned by rote."

The phrase, *"Their worship of me is nothing,"* is what we want to examine. It could mean at least 3 things:

1.   What they (we) do before coming to worship God -

 I AM ABRAHAM

Many People don't take God seriously. So, they come anyhow. Some come from their position or place of lying, fornication, anger, stealing, strifing, etc. Others come with their minds full of bitterness, unforgiveness, envy, jealousy, murder, etc. Some others too, come with doubt and unbelief. Some even come to God with idols in their hearts, they have alternative solutions in their minds, etc. I remember some years ago while still working in the secular. Two women came to me for prayers, and by God's grace, the following day the elderly one came testifying of the miracle God gave her. The other came confessing that nothing had happened because, in actual fact, her mind was not on the prayers. She went on to say that while I was praying, she was saying in her mind that I should finish quickly before the Chemist/Pharmacy shop would close!

2. What they (we) do when we are in God's presence - There are many things people do even in God's presence. Here, God said some irritate Him - they make Him angry or provoke His anger. In fact, their coming to His presence is an abomination to Him! As human beings, we are tripartite beings - we are made up of spirit, soul, and body. Many come to God's presence in worship (either personally, or corporately), yet they are not there. The body may be there physically but the mind and spirit are somewhere else. Even when the body is there physically, the parts of the body could be in a million places - the eyes, the ears, tongue, the hands, the mind - thoughts are preoccupied with much business. For some

APPROACHING GOD'S PRESENCE

people, it is the unfinished work or assignment that preoccupies them. For some, it is KFC, Post Office, e-mail or WhatsApp, Facebook, etc. Some others come to church to fight. We used to have a woman, all she does is to text and abuse people right in church while the service is going on! God said many of His people "honor Him with their lips, but their hearts are far from Him. And their worship of Him is nothing"! Does our worship have meaning with God? Does it move Him? Does it add value to us?

3. How they (we) leave God's presence - The coming of some people means nothing to God - it does not move Him. This is because they came without faith, without focus, and without expectations, so they go away empty-handed! (Hebrews 11:6; 12:2, Psalm 9:18; 62:5, Proverbs 10: 28; 11:23, Philippians 1:20). Some people came, but their faith is low - all they ask for is remnants and crumbs. Some specialize in asking for vanities, frivolities, rather than things that last - things that God Himself is concerned with like Kingdom issues, the perfect will of God, missions, the poor and needy, etc. (James 4:1-4, Matthew 6:13, 33, Mark 16:15-18). What does our faith take from God? What demands does our faith make on God? Does it take something big from God's treasury/storehouse, or do we leave Him untouched? (2 Kings 2: 9-15, Mark 5:2530, John 16:24).

In summary, whenever we are going into God's presence, don't let us go anyhow. Let us prepare and approach Him with reverence, and with a purpose. When preparing to approach God, what are we to do?:

(a) Know the One you are approaching – He is the Holy One of Israel (Exodus 15:11, Hebrews 12:28-29, Genesis 17:1, 1 Samuel 14:1-6, Isaiah 6:1-8, Revelation 1:1-8). Hence, sanctify yourself before coming near His presence.

(b) Enter His presence with thanksgiving and praise (Psalm 100:1-5) and purify yourself (Proverbs 28:13; Isaiah 55:6-7; 1 John 1:4-9, Psalm 15:1-5, Hebrews 4:16).

(c) Guard against every possible distraction and the distractors - whether from Satan, people, and things. We must learn to tune our senses to Heaven - close your eyes, see and hear God through every aspect of the moment/service. If there is any time the devil is mostly out to distract and make us lose focus, it is when we are in God's very presence!

Note: it is one thing to close one's eyes and another for the mind not to travel wide and wild!

The way to keep the mind from wandering is to set it on God - let it be set on great events, deeds, and acts in the Bible, or even some Biblical personalities that had faith, walked with God and did exploits for Him. Another way is to pay attention to the Scriptures mentioned (or which the Holy Spirit drops in our hearts). Of course, we are to get a jotter and pen nearby (for divine instructions).

It's time to pray:

Perhaps you are yet to have a personal relationship with Jesus. If this is so, then how does God expect you - a sinner to approach Him?:

"⁶ Seek the Lord while He may be found, Call upon Him while He is near. ⁷ Let the wicked forsake his way, And the unrighteous man his thoughts; Let him return to the Lord, And He will have mercy on him; And to our God, For He will abundantly pardon."... "¹³He who covers his sins will not prosper, But whoever confesses and forsakes them will have mercy."…. "⁹ Also He spoke this parable to some who trusted in themselves that they were righteous, and despised others: ¹⁰ "Two men went up to the temple to pray, one a Pharisee and the other a tax collector. ¹¹The Pharisee stood and prayed thus with himself, 'God, I thank You that I am not like other men—extortioners, unjust, adulterers, or even as this tax collector. ¹² I fast twice a week; I give tithes of all that I possess.' ¹³And the tax collector, standing afar off, would not so much as raise his eyes to heaven, but beat his breast, saying, 'God, be merciful to me a sinner!' ¹⁴ I tell you, this man went down to his house justified rather than the other; for everyone who exalts himself will be humbled, and he who humbles himself will be exalted." …"⁵ This is the message which we have heard from Him and declare to you, that God is light and in Him is no darkness at all. ⁶ If we say that we have fellowship with Him, and walk in darkness, we lie and

do not practice the truth. ⁷ But if we walk in the light as He is in the light, we have fellowship with one another, and the blood of Jesus Christ His Son cleanses us from all sin. ⁸ If we say that we have no sin, we deceive ourselves, and the truth is not in us. ⁹ If we confess our sins, He is faithful and just to forgive us our sins and to cleanse us from all unrighteousness." - (Isaiah 55:5-7, Proverbs 28:13, Luke 18:9-14; I John 1:5-9).

(See also, Proverbs 11:21, 23, Hebrews 10:27).

Prayer:

- Father, thank You that You are approachable.

- Father, please forgive me for not adequately preparing to come to Your presence.

- Father, whenever I have the privilege of coming to Your presence, don't let me go away empty-handed.

- Today, Father, please do a new thing in my life.

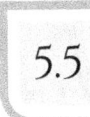

Spiritual Reading Of The Word

Here in this chapter, our focus will be on some principles of Bible reading or study.

In addition, we will see:

- The role of the Holy Spirit in helping us to understand the Word as we read.

- The concept of spiritual reading of the Bible

A. Some principles of Bible reading or study:

1. The Bible is to be read intentionally and deliberately. It is to be read with a definite purpose:

(a)　to know God,

(b)　to get food for our soul, and

(c)　to get instruction and direction from God.

 I Am Abraham

We are not to read the Bible as a past-time exercise. It's not something we do to while away the time or to "kill the time" as some people say.

2. We are to approach the Bible with prayer - looking for the Holy Spirit's guidance and illumination.

Also, we must:

a) have a definite time.

b) have a specific method – pray, read,

c) have a definite place – a quiet place/time.

d) Be prepared to obey the Word.

B. **The role of the Holy Spirit in helping us to understand the Word as we read:**

We Need the Holy Spirit to understand the Bible. Without His Help, it will just be like ordinary writing. All you will see will be letters and words.

"And we have such trust through Christ toward God. Not that we are sufficient of ourselves to think of anything as being from ourselves, but our sufficiency is from God, who also made us sufficient as ministers of the new covenant, not of the letter but of the Spirit; for the letter kills, but the Spirit gives life." 2 Corinthians 3:4-6

Hence, we need the help of the Holy Spirit (Psalm 119: 18; II Cor 2:9-11). The Holy Spirit can do a lot for us when, with His help, we read the Word of God. He can empower the Word so that the sanctifying power inherent in the Word can become operational in our lives:

" 17 Sanctify them by Your truth. Your word is truth. 18As You sent Me into the world, I also have sent them into the world. 19 And for their sakes I sanctify Myself, that they also may be sanctified by the truth."…. "16All Scripture is inspired by God and is useful to teach us what is true and to make us realize what is wrong in our lives. It corrects us when we are wrong and teaches us to do what is right. 17 God uses it to prepare and equip his people to do every good work." (John 17:17-19; II Tim 3:1617, NLT).

C. **The concept of spiritual reading of the Bible:**

(i) What does spiritual reading of the Scriptures entail? – it involves seeing/hearing with the eyes/ears and mind of the Holy Spirit as we go through the Scriptures. For these to happen,

* Before reading, there is need to pray and ask God to take over our whole being – our body, our soul, and our spirit (especially our mind)

* We must ask God to open our eyes of understanding (Psalm 119:18, Isaiah 55:1-3).

* And, very important too, we must get our pen and paper (a Notebook or Journal) ready.

* We must read and listen as the Holy Spirit invites your attention to words (nouns, verbs, adjectives, people, places, actions, etc.) in the passage.

It may be surprising to realize or know that God can speak to us through each word – the nouns, the verbs, the adjectives; the phrases, and events, etc in His Word - The Holy Bible. The Holy Spirit may even bring up people, places, issues, etc. in the past, present, and future, into your mind as you meditate in the Word.

* Watch out against distractions, infiltrations and interferences (it may be positive or negative - it may be of God, and it can be from the enemy (Isaiah 60:1-3, 1 Peter 5:7-9).

(ii) What spiritual reading of the Scriptures does - One of the things spiritual readings does is to guide against imputing the meanings God did not intend to His Word. For example, some people have ignorantly claimed and also preached that the five stones that David picked when he was going to confront Goliath signify the name of JESUS! Such people failed to realise that the Hebrew word transliterated as 'Jesus' - "YESHUA" has six letters.

I heard a pastor preaching too, sometime ago that the word "RCCG" (an acronym/name of a church denomination), is in the Bible. This he referred to Romans, I Corinthians, II Corinthians, and Galatians!

Spiritual Reading of the Scriptures help to curb all these frivolous imputations. Other Bible Verses that had been misused include Prov 18:16; Matt 11:12; Matt 19:14 (especially where the "suffereth" was used instead of "forbid").

(iii) Some practical guides to spiritual reading of the Scriptures - Pick a passage from the Bible. Pray and spend 5-10 minutes meditating on it. Write down what you believe the Holy Spirit is showing or saying to you. Then find someone to share or discuss it with.

By God's grace, in recent years God has made the spiritual reading of His Word part and parcel of my life, and I have been greatly enriched and mightily blessed. Nowadays, God has made it possible for me to apply it to any (and in fact everything) that has to do with my life.

For example, during my QUIET TIME (or personal devotion), or when doing my daily Bible reading, or even when preparing a Sermon the Holy Spirit quickens my understanding and expands God's word to me.

 I AM ABRAHAM

Let me share a few experiences here:

Daily Devotion - using Open Heavens (written by our father-in-the Lord, Pastor E. A. Adeboye): On many occasions, I have found myself spending close to one Hour in trying to digest and have the best from the day's topic and subject.

I start with a short prayer asking the Holy Spirit to open my eyes (Psalm 111:18). Then I try to do about five things:

(a) look at, think upon the topic or theme for the day,

(b) then take a look at and think upon the memory verse,

(c) thereafter I consider the Text for the day,

(d) then I go through the main issues raised in the Outline (in many cases, our Daddy will raise up to seven points),

(e) I conclude with the key/action point, and prayers.

The benefits of this daily experience had been unquantifiable to me. In addition to the fact that the Word of God gets expanded and expounded in my heart, the Word also sanctifies me, and guides my heart, my day, my life and my destiny. There is also a sense of peace, confidence and assurance that God is with me, and that

ALL will be well! [John 1:1-5; II Tim 3:16-17(NLT); Romans 8:28].

A typical Day with Open Heavens:

Topic: "When You Say 'Thank You Lord'" - II Chro 1:6-12; Memory Verse II Chro 1:7.

Short prayer (to start).

A deep look at the Topic - "When You Say 'Thank You Lord'"

The Word 'when' brings out some things: when, whenever, (as against "If").

The Word 'When' and it's uses (in the Scriptures):

- when I see the Blood, I will pass over you

- when a man's ways pleases the Lord, He will make his enemies to be at peace with him

- when the Lord turned the captivity of Zion, we were like them that dream.

Some songs also ran through my mind:

- when I think of the goodness of Jesus...

- when You come and collect Your people, remember me o Lord...

- when I remember He is coming again, I shout Halleluyah...

- when Jesus comes to reward His Servants....

"When you say 'Thank You'"

Some Questions could be asked: Who are we to (or should we) say 'thank you' to?; who can (or should) actually say 'Thank you'?; when are we to (or should we) say 'thank you'?; How can (or should we) say 'Thank you -' to people, and especially to God?

On the Memory Verse: *"On that night God appeared to Solomon, and said to him, "Ask! What shall I give you?"*

The words 'on', 'that', 'night', etc could be looked at very closely. But, let us look at the word 'night':

- 'Night' can refer to the night of a day, or of life, or of situations or circumstances.

- nights have some peculiarities: - little or no light, loneliness, sleep or rest. Also, several spiritual activities and transactions go on in the night (angels and demons, etc). There is also the good news:

- that nights don't make things dark before God (Psalm 139:11-12)!

- that no matter the type (category of night) a person is experiencing, God can appear, show up and speak - to encourage, direct, allay our fears, give us light, and make a way where there appeared to be none.

We can then turn to look at the Text for the day, and then the Outline. By the time God helps us to do all these, He may have also been stirring some prayer points in our hearts.

Two very critical habits that we need to form, cultivate and develop:

- the art of hearing, recognizing and heeding the Voice of God

- His presence - attracting, accessing, and carrying it with you everywhere you go.

The starting point - the pages of the Bible, let me illustrate: imagine that you receive letters from 5 people close to you. As you open each and read, whose voices do you hear in your mind? It's the same when you read the Bible: II Tim 3:16-17 (NLT). *"All scriptures is inspired by God and is useful to teach us what is true and to make us realize what is wrong in our lives. It corrects us when we are wrong and teaches us to do what is right. God uses it to prepare and prepare and equip his people to do every good work"*.

 I AM ABRAHAM

Note: As you cultivate the art of hearing and recognizing the Voice of God, expect attacks - distractions, from all angles - other voices - people, Satan, things, etc.

I - Isa 30:6: *"This Message came to me concerning..."*

* This - that, their, Then, these, they, this, those, thou, though, thus, thy,

* this message - from where, who, for who?

* what was the content of the message - direction, directive, warning, an answer to a question,

* came - how, when and where (while sleeping, walking, bathing, eating, reading the Bible, Praying?); from where, who, for who?

* Came to me - to me, to others (individual, family, organization, nations, churches, leaders, etc).

* Here, the message concerns: Who, what and where?

II Gen 45:4 *""Please, come closer," he said to them. So they came closer. And he said again, "I am Joseph, your brother, whom you sold into slavery in Egypt."*

Please - please, pleased, pleasers (men), pleasing, pleasure
Please - politeness, an appeal, courtesy.

Please let me; please help me; please see/take it/forgive me.

Pleased - happy/delighted with - *'This is my Beloved Son, in Whom I am well pleased'*.

Come closer -

Come - (opposite of go) - It is an invitation - come and see, come after, come before, come for, come here, come up, come down, come near, come with, come in, come out, come through, come from, come to, come into, or come together.

Please come - and help, take, receive, and start or intervene,

Please come nearer => they (Joesph's Brothers) were already close or near to some extent. Now, he is asking them to come closer. Who are you already close to? Do you need to get closer, stay far, or even separate yourself totally from them? Need to get closer to God - through His Word, in Prayers, obedience, in listening to His Voice.

Benefit of coming closer – see better, hear better and know better.

III - Genesis 46:3 *"I am God, the God of your father,"* the voice said. *"Do not be afraid to go down to Egypt, for there I will make your family into a great nation."*

* "I" - the Almighty I - I from Whom all "I"s derive their breath!

 I AM ABRAHAM

Today, there are 7.7 Billion people in our world, and all derive their breath from this great *"I am"*!

I am present continuous tense, Unchanged and Unchangeable, Ageless, Ever-present, etc. (Mal 3:6; Heb 13:8).

Implications:

* 'I am God' - because I don't change, and I am unchangeable, ageless, and ever present, I can do now, all I have ever done in the past, and even more! - All what I did in the past - since Creation, I can still do again today - my creative, restorative power is still intact - in the Universe. I can do or come through for you and your family.

Matters Arising:

* Are most people/dwellers on earth grateful to this great "I" for the breath of life He gave us?

* Are we using God's life in us for or against Him - for His glory or for ourselves (Rev 4:11)?

The breath He gave is on loan - one day, we will have to give account (Rom 14:12).

Prayer: Father, have mercy on me. Help me to be grateful to You. Help me to use Your life/breath in me for Your glory.

'I am God' - which God? - the God who created and sustains the Heaven and Earth; the God who rules and reigns in the affairs of men.

'I am God - the God of your father' -

- importance of fathers – physical or biological, and spiritual.
- who is my father? – physical or biological, and spiritual?

Who or what is the God (god) of my father(s)? - gods or the real, True and Living God?

'I am God - the God of your father' - Abraham, and Isaac.

The God of Abraham - covenant-keeping God; He is sovereign. He is the God who brings from obscurity to the limelight. He is that God "Who does not need the permission of anybody to make a nobody, Somebody!"

The God of Isaac - God of laughter – He can make people laugh; He can turn mourning to laughter; He can laugh at His enemies.

'The voice said' - the Voice here is the Voice of God - the 'First Voice' - priority Voice, the Final Voice.

What the Voice said here:

* I am God

* I am the God of your father

* Do/do not - What to do and not to do. What to be and not to be.

* Do not be afraid …

* Do not be afraid of …. (There are several things that can make us afraid - people, places, future, night, height, depth, death, etc).

* Do not be afraid to …. start, stop, move, give, receive,

* Do not be afraid to go … up, back, forward,

* Do not be afraid to go down … humble yourself, submit and give.

* Do not be afraid to go down to Egypt. Ordinarily, many things could make Jacob afraid of going down to Egypt.

Why must he (Jacob) not be afraid to go down to Egypt?

- because there (even there in Egypt), "I WILL MAKE YOUR FAMILY INTO A GREAT NATION"

- because Me (the Almighty God), have the power to turn 'the way down' to the way up! (the story of Joseph - from hatred or jealousy, to slavery, to prison, and from prison to the palace (Rom 8:28; Prov 19:21).

IV Isaiah 16:2 – "The women of Moab"

"The women of Moab are left like homeless birds at the shallow crossings of the Arnon River." (NLT)

- The women - Women in general. Special breed (chemistry, features, womb to carry babies, breast and milk to feed, menstrual flow - when it starts and stops - wisdom and greatness of God in display)

- Attributes of women – (positive and negative)

- Women I have known or pass through in life - at home, school, work, church, etc. Their impact/influence, what to remember/never forget or what to never remember about them.

- The women of Moab, Canaan, Philistines, Egypt, Israel, Nigeria (Ibo, Yoruba, Hausa, Calabar, Itshekiri, etc.) – the general stereotypes about them!

- The women of Moab - What they carry (the DNA of Lot and his first daughter - the spirit of Sodom, Incest, homosexual, lesbianism, Gay, etc. The need to watch against stereotypes about women - because one may be different - either for good or for evil! For example, a particular Moabite woman that stood out in history - RUTH!)

- The Moabite women are left - Who left them? Where and what were they left to do? When were they left? Was it at the time when they desperately needed help? Men (friends, relations, husbands, employers, leaders, society, etc) could leave us. Who must not leave a man – God! Yet, God can leave a man! Consider examples of people that God left in the Bible, and how they ended (Judges 16:16-25; I Samuel 16:13-16; Hos. 4:17, 5:9-11).

(D) How does the spiritual reading affect and shape a person's life?

"Oh, how I love Your law! It is my meditation all the day." Psalm 119:97

If, for example, what you read and mediated upon on a day is Isaiah 16:2, (as we did above here), how will it affect your day? Look out for women and probably appreciate God for all about them, watch out for different behaviors from women (both good and not so good). You could imagine/think of the spirits that make some women do what they do. Would you be angry, flare up or lose your temper? Not likely?

 AFTERWORDS

As I began to round off the materials for this autobiography, the Bible story of Joseph once again came vividly to my mind, especially the journey of the young man to the top. It was a dream come true!

In Genesis 37:5-11 (NLT), God had given Joseph two successive dreams of greatness:

" ⁵*One night Joseph had a dream, and when he told his brothers about it, they hated him more than ever.* ⁶*"Listen to this dream," he said.* ⁷*"We were out in the field, tying up bundles of grain. Suddenly my bundle stood up, and your bundles all gathered around and bowed low before mine!"* ⁸*His brothers responded, "So you think you will be our king, do you? Do you actually think you will reign over us?" And they hated him all the more because of his dreams and the way he talked about them.* ⁹*Soon Joseph had another dream, and again he told his brothers about it. "Listen, I have had another dream," he said. "The sun, moon, and eleven stars bowed low before me!"* 10*This time he told the dream to his father as well as to his brothers, but his father scolded him.*

"What kind of dream is that?" he asked. "Will your mother and I and your brothers actually come and bow to the ground before you?" ¹¹But while his brothers were jealous of Joseph, his father wondered what the dreams meant."

There were, of course, several things associated with the dreams that were not shown to him, or that were not so clear at that time. For example, in the second dream, Joseph saw eleven stars, with the sun and moon bowing down to him. His father, Jacob, thought that in addition to Joseph's eleven brothers, the sun and moon meant that he and his wife - mother (Rachel) too were one day going to bow down to Joseph.

As things turned out later, it was never recorded in the Bible that Jacob and Rachel (who in fact, may have died not too long after the dreams), ever bowed down to their son Joseph. However, the brothers did. They bowed to the ground at least not less than four times! What then did the sun and the moon represent or stand for? I believe they had to do with where Joseph's dreams would eventually be fulfilled - a foreign land where the sun and moon were worshipped. Egypt perfectly fits this description.

In Egypt, several gods and goddesses were worshipped – about 2,000 of them! One of these gods/goddesses was called "Khosu" – the god of the moon who also loved gambling. It was said that this god was venerated as the

 I AM ABRAHAM

Deity of Moon – the god of the Moon! Another Egyptian god was called "Aten (Ra)" – the sun god, the supreme lord of the gods, held to be the creator of the universe and human beings.

In Gen 41:41-43, the Bible recorded that after Pharaoh had appointed Joseph his Assistant (or the Prime Minister), everywhere Joseph went, the command was shouted;

"Bow the kneel..." Finally, and at last, Egypt and her gods, particularly Khonsu and Aten (Ra), bowed to Joseph (Numbers 23:19, Isaiah 40:8).

An additional lesson here, is that when God speaks, He will do what He says, no matter how remote it seemed.

To get Joseph to the top in Egypt, the Almighty God tremendously used Joseph's brothers. Though what they did to Joseph was unpleasant and very painful, yet without that Joseph would never have reached the top in Egypt. It appeared this truth also dawned on Joseph. Hence, we read in Genesis 45:1-8 (NLT):

" ¹Joseph could stand it no longer. There were many people in the room, and he said to his attendants, "Out, all of you!" So he was alone with his brothers when he told them who he was. ²Then he broke down and wept. He wept so loudly the Egyptians could hear him, and word of it quickly carried to Pharaoh's palace. ³"I am Joseph!" he said to his brothers. "Is my father still alive?" But

> his brothers were speechless! They were stunned to realize that Joseph was standing there in front of them. ⁴"Please, come closer," he said to them. So they came closer. And he said again, "I am Joseph, your brother, whom you sold into slavery in Egypt. ⁵But don't be upset, and don't be angry with yourselves for selling me to this place. It was God who sent me here ahead of you to preserve your lives. ⁶This famine that has ravaged the land for two years will last five more years, and there will be neither plowing nor harvesting. ⁷God has sent me ahead of you to keep you and your families alive and to preserve many survivors. ⁸So it was God who sent me here, not you! And he is the one who made me an adviser to Pharaoh—the manager of his entire palace and the governor of all Egypt."

Another personality that God used for Joseph was Mrs. Potiphar. Her lies landed Joseph in prison, and it was there (in prison) he met the man who eventually recommended him as an accurate "dream decoder" to Pharaoh.

In becoming who I am in life, I have had several "Brothers of Joseph," as well as some "Mrs. Potiphars" in my life! Today, I thank God for all their roles in my life. At the time they were "peppering" my life, it was very painful. But looking back now, it is clear that God in His infinite wisdom put them there. I thank them all. I hold no grudge against any of them, anymore! They meant evil, but God had turned them all to my good:

"¹⁸Then his brothers came and threw themselves down before Joseph. "Look, we are your slaves!" they said. ¹⁹But Joseph replied, "Don't be afraid of me. Am I God, that I can punish you? ²⁰You intended to harm me, but God intended it all for good. He brought me to this position so I could save the lives of many people. ²¹No, don't be afraid. I will continue to take care of you and your children." So he reassured them by speaking kindly to them. ²²So Joseph and his brothers and their families continued to live in Egypt. Joseph lived to the age of 110." Genesis 50:18-22 (NLT)

" ²⁸ And we know that God causes everything to work together for the good of those who love God and are called according to his purpose for them. ²⁹ For God knew his people in advance, and he chose them to become like his Son, so that his Son would be the firstborn among many brothers and sisters. ³⁰ And having chosen them, he called them to come to him. And having called them, he gave them right standing with himself. And having given them right standing, he gave them his glory. ³¹ What shall we say about such wonderful things as these? If God is for us, who can ever be against us?" Romans 8:28-31 (NLT).

TO GOD BE THE GLORY!

Bible Study Outlines

Included in this Section are Bible Study Outlines on three core areas:

| 01 | UNDERSTANDING GOD,

| 02 | RELASED INTO DESTINY,

| 03 | BEHOLD HE COMETH.

Most of the Outlines came and were originally developed as teaching and resource materials. In addition, at the end of the book, there are some Personal Growth Hints, that will definitely bless everyone.

UNDERSTANDING GOD

General Introduction

Three concepts are often discussed together. These are: knowledge, understanding, and wisdom. The reason is because the three are interrelated, and in fact one leads to the other.

Knowledge, among other things, has been defined as:

- the fact or condition of knowing something, with familiarity gained through experience or association;

- the fact or condition of being aware of something, the range of one's information or understanding;

- the circumstance or condition of apprehending truth or fact through reasoning;

- the fact or condition of having information or of being learned;

- the sum of what is known: the body of truth, information, and principles acquired by humankind

Understanding:

- a mental grasp, or COMPREHENSION

- the power of comprehending;

- the power to make experience intelligible by applying concepts and categories

- a mutual agreement not formally entered into but in some degree binding on each side

- friendly or harmonious relationship;

- An agreement of opinion or feeling: adjustment of differences

Wisdom:

- The ability to discern inner qualities and relationships, also referred to as INSIGHT

- good sense: JUDGMENT

Knowledge is power. Understanding is of a superior power. It is not enough to have some basic information about a thing, it is critical to also know the intricacies or outworking of the object of information.

It is when we now apply both correctly, that we are said to be wise.

In the Bible Book of Proverbs, two Chapters (8 and 24), are devoted to benefits of wisdom, and in effect, the terrible dangers of foolishness or a lack of wisdom.

Knowing God, and understanding how He operates will greatly make our lives easier, less complicated, and our life endeavours very fruitful.

Having pointed out the link between knowledge, understanding, and wisdom, in this Series, the theme "UNDERSTANDING GOD" will therefore be looked at from two perspectives:

*   Knowledge of God, and

*   Understanding God

KNOWLEDGE OF GOD I

1. Importance of Knowledge

2. The Utmost Knowledge

1. Importance of Knowledge: Knowledge is Power! What a man knows (or refuses to know) can make or unmake him

"Then Jesus said to those Jews who believed Him, "If you abide in My word, you are My disciples indeed. And you shall know the truth, and the truth shall make you free."...Therefore if the Son makes you free, you shall be free indeed." (John 8:31-32, 36)

Ignorance is the opposite of knowledge, and ignorance can be very dangerous!

"My people are destroyed for lack of knowledge. Because you have rejected knowledge, I also will reject you from being priest for Me; Because you have forgotten the law of your God, I also will forget your children. "The more they increased, The more they sinned against Me; I will change their glory into shame."

NLT: *"My people are being destroyed because they don't know me. Since you priests refuse to know me, I refuse to recognize you as my priests. Since you have forgotten the laws of your God, I will forget to bless your children. Hosea 4:7 The more priests there are, the more they sin against me. They have exchanged the glory of God for the shame of idols."* (Hosea 4:6-7, NKJV).

From this passage, it is clear too that there is nothing more dangerous than to be a lost sheep under a lost shepherd!

Part of the dangers of ignorance is that it can make you to be at ease in Zion (even when there is fire on the mountain)! In addition, when a person is ignorant, he/she can mistake an enemy for a friend (and vice versa).

Ignorance can also lead to abuse, and premature death.

Hence the need to seek knowledge - the right knowledge!

2. The Utmost Knowledge: The most important knowledge to seek is the knowledge of God - it is The Utmost knowledge.

"Thus says the Lord: "Let not the wise man glory in his wisdom, Let not the mighty man glory in his might, Nor let the rich man glory in his riches; But let him who glories glory in this, That he understands and knows Me, That I am the Lord, exercising lovingkindness, judgment, and righteousness in the earth. For in these I delight," says the Lord." Jer 9:23-24 (See also Phil 3:7-14).

- Where can we find the true and accurate knowledge of God?

There is only one answer to this Question: in His Word - the Holy Bible!

There are many benefits of Discovering God through His Word. One of such benefits is that it will help you to also discover yourself. *"All scripture is inspired by God and is useful to teach us what is true and to make us realize what is wrong in our lives. It corrects us when we are wrong and teaches to do what is right. God uses it to prepare and equip his people to do every good work."* 2 Tim. 3:16-17 (NLT)

Furthermore, you will be equipped to recognize counterfeit and fake Christians, false teachers, false prophets, and the evil people who are misrepresenting God.

In addition to all these, you will realize that there is no one who can really surprise you anymore! Why? It is because you will realize that men can do anything, I mean anything - both good and evil - whether black or white, yellow or green! This means that you won't develop High Blood Pressure, or be anxious about anything (Phil 4:6-8, NLT)

The ONLY ONE who can surprise us is God. This is because He can intervene in very unusual ways (Psalm 89:1, 22-24; Psalm 124:1-8; Psalm 91-5-10).

Proverbs 9:10 declares:

"The fear of the Lord is the beginning of wisdom, and the knowledge of the holy is understanding"

KNOWLEDGE OF GOD II

1. The God who is alive

2. The Nature and Character of God

3. A God of purpose and Principles

1. The God who is alive:

The God of the Bible is a Living God. He is not a force, or an imaginary thing. He is real. He is alive.

One of the valid evidences that something is real and alive is that it can speak, make sound, and can move if need be. For example, plants, birds, man, even the engine of a car, etc.

The same is true of God – the God of the Bible. One of the purest evidences that God is real, and that He is alive is that He speaks - He is a speaking God (Psalm 94:1-14; Rom 1:18-21).

When God speaks, it could be:

- * to call you by your very name - (Luke 19:5; John 21:15-17).

- * to give direction (Acts 10:1-6, 19-24).

- * to warn (Prove 28:13; Rom 6:23).

- * to allay your fears - Isa 41:10-13;

- * to give you assurance (Isa 1:19; Isa 3:10; Psalm 30:5).

- * to dialogue - He could ask you a question, or be answering your own questions. For example:

- He asked Adam and wife: Where are you? (Gen 3:9-11)

- He asked Ezekiel: son of man, Can these bones live? (Ezek. 37:1-10)

- He is asking you, even now – you who are still living in sin, and yet want God to help you: Shall we continue in sin and expect the grace of God to continue? - God forbid!(Rom 6:1-2)

- He asked Jeremiah: Is there anything too hard for Me? (Jer 32:27)

- He asked all tithe defaulters: Will a man rob God? (Mal 3:8-12)

- He asked Bartimaeus, the blind man: What do you want Me to do for you? (Mark 10:46-52).

There are many things to know about God (Jer 9:23-24; Daniel 11:32c). These include:

His Person; His Purpose (and Plans); His principles; His power; etc.

Let us now look at these in some details.

2. The Nature and Character of God (His personality):

* God - who is He? - a Living (Daniel 4:1-5, 33-37), Holy (Lev 19:1-2; I Peter 1:15-16; Heb 12:4); Loving (John 3:16-18; John 15:13); Merciful (Psalm 89:1-3; Psalm 136:1-end); and Faithful God (I Kings 8:56; Psalm 89:1-3; I Cor 2:9).

* The All-knowing God - Acts 15:18

* The Alpha and Omega - Rev 1:8,18

* The All-seeing God - (I Sam 18:7; Matt 6:4, 6; Psalm 139:1-12)

* The God Who hears - (Num 14:27-34; Jer 33:3)

* The God Who speaks - Gen 1:1-3. A common or recurring phrase in Gen 1, is 'And God said' or 'And God called', or 'And God saw'.

* The God who handles - He has Hands (left and right), Isa 59:59; Jesus is seated on the right Hand of God.

* The God who moves - By this we mean His Acts and interventions on the earth - in the affairs of mankind (Psalm 92:1-5). He moves and removes people and situations.

* The God who lives and reigns forever - Rev 1:18-20

3. **The God of Purpose and Principles:** Purpose is the reason why something exists or the reason why something is done. In many cases purposes are hidden and are waiting to be discovered.

Another word that can be used for purpose is 'motives'. As human beings because the heart can't easily be unveiled, motives are not easy to discern. People can tell you why they do what they do. But the real motives and or purpose may be hidden for long (Jer 17:9). God is different from man! (Num 23:19).

An adage says - 'When purpose is not known, abuse is inevitable'. If there is any area where this is more true, it is in human lives. Because many are ignorant of God's purpose, they abuse themselves and abuse others - spouses, children, employees, systems, resources (stories: - of Joseph's Brothers; Saul of Tarsus; the man who God gave a wonderful woman to as wife, but beats her!).

God and Purpose: God is a God of great purposes. He doesn't do a thing except for a purpose

He made us for a purpose Gen 1:26-28; Rev 4:11; Within the grand (ultimate) purpose of God, there are sub-purposes.

For example, within the grand purpose for which He made man, God has some stages every man must pass through. Each stage is to serve an aspect of the grand purpose. In the end, He expects that the ultimate purpose is (or should) be fulfilled.

Still talking about sub-purposes, if we look at human beings, after we are born, we go to school, have a career, get married, and we start a new cycle of life and family. Attached to God's purpose are plans, people, places, and opportunities.

KNOWLEDGE OF GOD III
THE POWER OF GOD

The Power of God:

The God of the Bible - the Lord God of Israel, is a God of unlimited power (Gen 17:1; Jer 32:26-27; Luke 1:37). Three things inform or determine how God operates His power: His character (holiness and integrity), His principles, and His purpose (II Tim 2:19; Prov 19:21; Lam 3:37).

We have already looked at the Character, the principles for, and the purposes of God. Let us now see how these affect (or determine) how God exercises His power:

*   His character (and integrity) - God exercises His power in line with His Holy and Righteous character. He won't do something that will make man to accuse Him of partiality or unfairness (Gen 18:25; Acts 10:34-35; II Tim 2:19)

*   His principles - (Gen 8:20-22; Gal 6:6-8).

*   His purpose - (Prov 19:21; Lam 3:37).

One may want to ask: "How powerful is God?: I believe that a look at the dimensions of His power will answer this question.

(a)   God is the Almighty. He is also Sovereign - (Gen 17:1; Luke 1:37) -

What does His Almightiness and Sovereignty mean?:

By Sovereignty, we mean:

*   God is superior and Supreme - He is greater than all, and He is above all.

*   God can do anything (Psalm 115:3). However, He is not arbitrary - He works by principles.

*   God can use anything, anywhere, and at any time to achieve His desires, His purposes, and His plans.

*   God has the final or last say in all matters. This simply means that when He says Yes, no man can say No. When He opens, no one can close. When He has not said a matter is over, the chapter is not yet closed. When He says you will live, even when the enemy has tried to put you in the grave, my Father can open the grave and bring you out! (Rev 3:7-8; Jn 11:38-44)

*   God does not see as men see (I Sam 16:7; Matt 6:4,6).

*   God is the King of all kings, as well as the Lord of all lords. This implies that He appoints Kings, and it is He alone who can secure and protect them.

God rules, and He can overrule or override the decisions of any (and all) kings!

He determines the tenure of kings. He can terminate, remove, and replace them if, and when the need arises.

(b)   God is also the Man of War – a God who fights! - He can fight for, and defend His people (II Chron 20:12-24).

(c)   God is the Great Deliverer - The God who defends. He defends His Word, His people, His Covenant (Gen 17:1-16)

(d)   God is the Great Restorer – He can restore losses, relationships, health, and destinies (Psalm 126:1-3)

(e)   God is the unstoppable God – Nothing - no one, and no power can stop or slow down God. Whatever a person tries to do - whether directly or indirectly to stop God, may ultimately, in fact be fast-tracking

God's Plan! We see this vividly in the lives of people like Joseph – (Gen. 45:1-8); Moses - (Exod 2:1-10), etc.

"And we know that all things work together for good to those who love God, to those who are the called according to His purpose." (Rom 8:28).

KNOWLEDGE OF GOD IV
THE INTEGRITY OF THE WORD OF GOD

The integrity of the Word of God – THE HOLY BIBLE.

The term "The Word of God" can have about three connotations:

* What God said directly - and was heard, written, documented as His voice or word;

* What He is said to have said – that is, what was credited to Him.

* Jesus - the Living Word of God.

The power in the Word of a person is a function of his or her net worth - the physical assets, liquidity in banks, and his or her goodwill - (his or her integrity and legacy, Prov 22:1; Eccles 7:1).

The same with God! The power of His Word is a function of His net worth. The Question then is: How much does God worth? (Psalm 24:1-2; Psalm 8:1-2; Haggai 2:6-8; Psalm 50:10-15).

God and His Word. There are a lot the Bible has said about the Word of God. Scriptural passages like Heb 4:12; 2 Tim 3:16-17; Rom 4:21; Psalm 33:8-12; Num 23:19; Isa 40:8; Isa 55:1011; Jer 1:12; Psalm 119:89; John 6:63; Isa 46:3-13, are among such.

Since it is in the Word of God - the Holy Bible that we find all there is to know about God, it is critical that anyone who sincerely wants to know God and please Him should as a matter of necessity make studying Gods Word his or her preoccupation.

Activity – Case Study:

(a)   Joseph (Gen 37:5-11; Gen 45:1-8)

(i)   Identify God's purpose, the plan, people, and places.

*   What helped Joseph to eventually fulfill God's purpose?

*   What are the things that could have prevented the ultimate Purpose of God in Joseph's life?

- * Applying Joseph's story to your own life:

- (ii) Can you identify God's purpose, the plan, people, and places in your own life?

- * What has been helping you, or can help you to eventually fulfill God's purpose for your life?

- * What are the things that could prevent the ultimate Purpose of God in your life?

- * What are you going to do to help you fulfill the purpose of God for your life?

- (b) JESUS:

- (John 3:3, 16-18; Matt 1:18-21; John 14:6; Acts 4:11-13)

- His principles (Psalm 115:3; Isa 55:8-9).

UNDERSTANDING GOD - PART I: THE FEAR OF THE LORD

Text: Psalm 112:1-3

Introduction: This new series is on GOD – THE ALMIGHTY. I believe HE is the most important personality we need to know about, and who we can never know too much about. May He continue to reveal Himself to us more and more in Jesus Name, Amen.

This first Part will be on "The Fear of The Lord"

OUTLINE:

1. The Fear of the Lord

2. A Divine Enabler

3. The Fear of the Lord - A Necessity

Text (Psalm 112:1-3):

"Praise the Lord! Blessed is the man who fears the Lord, Who delights greatly in His commandments. His descendants will be mighty on earth; The generation of the upright will be blessed. Wealth and riches will be in his house, And his righteousness endures forever."

1. The Fear of the Lord: The Word 'Fear' appeared in several places in the Scriptures. We are asked not to fear some things or some people. However, we are strictly commanded to fear God. Perhaps one of the problems we have in the world, (and even the church) today is that men no longer seem to fear God. Deut. 3:2; Deut. 6:2; Deut. 10:12; I Sam 12:13-16; Rom 8:14-16; II Tim 1:7; Prov 9:10; Prov 14:16; 26-27; Prov 16:6; Acts 10:34-35; I Sam 12:24;

*** A frequent command given to God's people in the OT is to "fear God" or "fear the Lord." It is important that we understand what this command means for Christ's followers today. Only as we truly fear the Lord will we be freed from all destructive and satanic fears. By fearing God, we can avoid being trapped by the natural pull toward going our own way, defying God and giving in to the inviting ways of immoral behavior.

2.   A Divine Enabler: The Fear of God, like Grace is a divine Enabler. It bestows us with abilities to do some things and also to refrain from some things. The fear of God will make you stay far from evil. It will also make you untouchable to all evil. The fear of God expels all other fears. Gen 14:1-8; Gen 22:12; Gen 39:7-9; Exod 1:17-18; I Sam 24: 1-10; II Kings 17:39; I Chro 14:17.

3.   The Fear of the Lord - A Necessity: The fear of the Lord is far more than a Biblical teaching, principle or idea. It is relevant to our daily lives in many ways. Hence, we must ask God to plant His fear in our heart. Prov 8:13; Acts 10:3435; Isa 66:1-2; Psalm 33:6-9; Psalm 96:4-5; John 1:9; Exo. 20:18-20; Eccl 3:14; John 1:11-16; Mark 4:39-41; Rev 15:4; Matt 17:1-8; Psalm 130:4; I Sam 12:24; Psalm 34:9; Psalm 67:7.

*** Above all, the fact that the Lord is a God of justice - the One Who will judge the entire human race - should be reason enough to produce a godly fear It is a sobering and absolute truth that God is constantly aware of our actions and motives, both good and bad, and that we will be held accountable for those actions, both now and on the day of our personal judgment. (Deut. 17:12-13; Isa 59: 18-19; Mal 3:5; Heb 10:26-31).

*** In Daniel 11:32, the Bible says:

KJV- *"Those who do wickedly against the covenant he shall corrupt with flattery; but the people who know their God shall be strong, and carry out great exploits."*

NLT - *"He will flatter and win over those who have violated the covenant. But the people who know their God will be strong and will resist him."*

The part we love to quote is: "the people who know their God shall be strong, and carry out great exploits." There is another side to it: "the people who know their God shall fear Him and flee evil." (Like the man Job - the Bible said he feared God and shunned evil". (One version said "He was a man of complete integrity, and He feared God and stayed away from evil."

Conclusion: God loves us. He wants us to fear Him, and not take Him for granted. It is a wise thing to fear God. It is highly rewarding to fear Him. May He help us to truly fear Him and also begin to enjoy the blessings He has prepared for those who fear Him in Jesus Name.

Prayers:

- Father, thank You for Who You are (Acts 10:34). Please help me to truly know and fear You.

- Father, please plant Your fear in my hear, let nothing take Your fear out of me

- Father, please bring back Your fear into Your Church - help us (both leaders and followers) to truly fear You.

UNDERSTANDING GOD - PART II: THE FEAR OF THE LORD (A)

Text: Psalm 128:1-6

Introduction: In part 1 of this series, we saw among other things, what it means to fear the Lord, and the necessity of His fear. We also saw what the fear of God could enable us to do or restrain us from doing. As we continue, we will be focusing on some of the blessings that go with the fear of the Lord. May the Lord make us partakers of these blessings in Jesus Name. Amen!

OUTLINE:

1.   Those who know God, also Fear Him!

2.   It pays to Fear God

1. Those who know God, also Fear Him: Those who don't fear God, or who take Him for granted do so because they don't really know God! Anyone who truly knows God would fear Him! The true knowledge of God instills fear in those who know Him. Exo. 5:1-3; Exo. 8:19; Exo. 12:29-33; Rom 9:16-17; Luke 18:1-8; Lev 25:17; Daniel 11:32; Job 28:28.

*** In the Book of Exod 7:14, (all through to the end of Exod 14), we see God showing a little of Himself.

2. It pays to Fear God: In whatever way it is looked at, it pays to fear the Lord. Nothing else seem to attract more blessings than the fear of God. Psalm 112:1; Deut 6:24; I Sam 12;14-15; II Kings 17:24-28; I Chron 14:17; Job 28:28; Psalm 25:14; Psalm 33:18; Psalm 33:8; Psalm 34:7; Psalm 103:17; Psalm 115:11; Jer 5:24; Eccles 8:12-13; Psalm 128:1-6.

*** Point out the various blessings listed in the main Text (Psalm 128:1-6 NKJV): *"Blessed is every one who fears the Lord, Who walks in His ways. When you eat the labor of your hands, You shall be happy, and it shall be well with you. Your wife shall be like a fruitful vine. In the very heart of your house, Your children like olive plants All around your table. Behold, thus shall the man be blessed Who fears the Lord. The Lord bless you out of Zion, And may you see the good of Jerusalem All the days of your life. Yes, may you see your children's children. Peace be upon Israel!"*

Conclusion: Since we have now known that it pays to fear God, as we determine to fear Him, may He too honour His promises in our lives in Jesus Name.

Prayers:

- Father, as I too fear You, pour upon me all the blessings You promised to those who fear You.

- Father, in all I do or say, let Your fear guide me.

- Every problem that my lack of Your fear had brought into my life, Father, please remove them today.

UNDERSTANDING GOD - PART III
THE FEAR OF GOD (B)

Text: Psalm 23:1-6

Introduction: In this concluding part on The Fear of God we shall be looking at other fears, as well as the role of Conscience in the fear of God. May the Lord wake up our conscience unto righteousness.

OUTLINE:

1. There are other Fears!

2. Conscience and the Fear of God

1. There are other Fears: There are other fears besides the Fear of God! However, anyone who truly fears God has nothing else to fear Psalm 23:4; Isa 41: 10-13. The devil is the one behind every other fear (besides the fear of God). Several times in the Bible, we are commanded not to give room in our heart to such other fears. Rom 8:14-15; II Tim

 I Am Abraham

1:7; Psalm 91:5, 15-16; Gen 26:24; Gen 35:17; Num 21:34; Deut. 1:21; Deut. 3:2, 22; Joshua 10:8; Judges 6:10; II Kings 17:35; I Sam 22:23; II Kings 6:16; I Chro 28:20; Psalm 46:2; Psalm 56:4; Ezra 2:6; Jer 42:11; Jer 10:5Isa 10:24; Prov 3:25; Psalm 49:16; II Kings 19:6; II Chro 32:7.

*** In many places in the Bible we see God asking His people 'not to fear them' - included in the "them" are: men, enemies, and the gods of the heathen Nations - which are not God but mere works of men - with eyes that cannot see, hands that cannot move, and mouths that cannot speak!

2. Conscience and the Fear of God:

*** "Conscience"- definitions and usages

- a faculty, power, or principle enjoining good acts

- one's internal sense of right and wrong (principles, values, standards, morality, etc)

- a sensitive regard for fairness or justice

God has put this "sense of right and wrong" in everyone He created. It is sin that silences, makes us insensitive, or even kills it! When we are genuinely born again, the Holy Spirit makes our internal sense of right and wrong to come alive. That's why we are then sensitive to doing what is right, and we flee from what is wrong. When we claim to be a Christian, or even a Minister, and we do evil (unbiblical things), and we don't feel bad, then our consciences are dead! Where can we get help? - go back to God - confess to Him, and ask Him in His mercy to wake up our conscience - make it come alive again. (SEE Ephes 2:1-10 NLT).

Conclusion: Let us look into our lives - Who has the devil been using, or what has he been capitalizing upon to create fear, or harass you? Confront them today, and receive permanent victory in Jesus Name (II Cor 10:3-4; Psalm 56:3-4; James 4:6-7; Rev 12:11).

Prayer:

1. Father, please plant Your fear (Prov. 8:13).

2   Father, as I fear You, please uproot every other fear from me (Prov. 28:1).

3. Father, by Your word and Holy Spirit, please keep my conscience alive (Acts 24:16).

UNDERSTANDING GOD - PART IV
THE LOVE OF GOD

Text: John 3:16-18

Introduction: We thank God for our discussions on the 'The Fear of God'. I pray that His fear will remain in our heart and will propel us to always seek to please God. As we continue the general Theme: *"UNDERSTANDING GOD"*, we want to look at another attribute of God - Love. May the Holy Spirit Visit us in Jesus Name, AMEN.

OUTLINE:

1.   The Love of God

2.   The Love for God

The Love of God: That God loves us is unquestionable! He has demonstrated it in several ways. Central to everything God does, is His love for man. God's love is however purposeful! He loves us so that He can draw us out of our lost condition to Himself. When God loves a man, there is no extent He cannot go to demonstrate it. In fact, He can do anything for the one He loves. John 3:16-18; John 15:13; Rom 5:6-8; Ephes 2:1-13; I Sam 16:1-16; Psalm 89:1, 16-35; II Sam 12:24-25; I Chro 29:18-25; I Kings 11:1-11; Ephes 2:110, 11-19; John 17:1-5.

*** A great man of God testified of his conversation: "Jesus appeared to me, and I recognized Him as my Saviour. 'Tell us sir, what Jesus looked like!' 'Love' - 'can you see it?' 'No! Yet it's so real - that people can do anything to have it, and can do anything for lack (or denial) of it!"

*** Love of God

- God's type of love - agape love - unconditional. Loving the unlovable, loving a sworn enemy (Romans 5:6-8; John 3:16-18)

- a model and standard for love (i.e, loving like God does) - we have to receive a Heart like His own before we can. An heart transplant must occur.

The Love for God: By this we mean the love for God as well as things that pertain to Him. God wants us to have a genuine heart for Him (and everything that pertains to Him). This should be one of the ways of reciprocating His love for us. Among the things God would want us to focus our love for Him upon are: His Word and Truth; His

Name; His House on earth; People (all creatures, the Nation of Israel, Christians, His Servants/Ministers); His Kingdom and everything that will enhance its expansion (Missions and Missionaries, Church planting, Evangelism, Church Projects, etc); His ultimate home - Heaven, we must do all we can to get there!

Psalm 1:1-3; Psalm 119:89, 105, 130; Psalm 27:4-John 8:32, 36; Exo. 20:7; Prov 18:10; Gen 12:1-3; Psalm 105:12-16; Matt 6:33; Rom 10:12-15; Rom 12:1-2; Dan 12:3; Heb 12:14; Luke 10:17-20.

*** Love for God: love that is focused on Him and all that pertains to Him.

Conclusion: God loves you. Do you love Him? If you value His love, how have you been showing it? (John 14:15).

Prayers:

1. Father, thank You for your Love, please help me to truly love you (Jn. 14:15).

2. Father, increase my love for the things you love, particularly souls (Jn. 3:16).

3. Father, please keep me in your love to the very end (Rev. 22:10-12).

UNDERSTANDING GOD - PART V
THE LOVE OF GOD

Text: Deut. 11:13-25

Introduction: In our previous study, we saw all that love made God to do for us. We also noted that God expects us to reciprocate His love by loving Him in return. As we continue, we shall look at the subject in more details. May the Holy Spirit speak to us in Jesus Name, Amen.

1. The Command to love

2. Love is Purposeful

1. The Command to love: Obeying the command to love (both God and Man), is basic to us as God's children. It is to reciprocate God's love for us. It is also a demonstration of His nature in us. There are several things we can do to express our love to God and to man. Of course, there are many things we can do too to show we love people - we can care - share our time and goods; we can warn against dangers (physical and spiritual); we can protect, we can render regular and uncommon services, etc. (Deut. 6:4-9; Heb 1:9; Matt 22:37-39; Mark 12:28-31; Luke 10:27; James 2:8-13, 14-17; Luke 10:25-40; Luke 11:5-8).

Also earlier, we looked at some of the things God would want us to focus our love for Him upon. Our attitude and what to do in each of these areas - the interest, energy and commitment we show to these things will tell Him how much we love what He too loves and cherished. These include: His Word and Truth; His Name; His House on earth; People (all creatures, the Nation of Israel, Christians, His Servants/Ministers); His Kingdom and everything that will enhance its expansion (Missions and Missionaries, Church planting, Evangelism, Church Projects, etc); His ultimate home - Heaven, we must do all we can to get there!

2. **Love is Purposeful:** Demonstrating or expressing Love is purposeful. Central to God's love for man is our redemption, and He did all He could to realize that goal. Our ultimate purpose as we too share God's love with men, should be to bring them to God. If they already knew God, ours should make them to love Him more. Love is rewarding. When we truly love, it means we are becoming like our Heavenly Father. The ultimate reward of love is that we will reign with Jesus forever. John 3:16-18; John

1:11-13; John 15:13; Heb 12:1-3; Rom 16:1-20; Eph. 2:5-8; I John 3:1-3.

Conclusion: Be an example of a true Believer. Love purposefully!

Prayers:

- Father, make me a lovable person.

- Father, please teach and empower me to love You, and love others - both children of God and even Unbelievers.

- Father, help me to love purposefully.

UNDERSTANDING GOD - PART VI
THE WILL & MIND OF GOD

Text: Matt 6:5-18

Introduction: Today, we are moving into another area of our series on *"Understanding God"*. There is nothing that can give rest to a soul as having assurance that one is in the prefect will of God, and one is operating according to the mind of God. In this Study, may the Holy Spirit make clear to us, both the will and the mind of God as the need arises in Jesus Name, AMEN.

OUTLINE:

1. The Will versus The Mind of God

2. God still Guides His own

1. The Will versus The Mind of God: God is a good and loving Father. He made us for some definite purposes. He is more than prepared to bare His mind on what He has in store for us. Very often, we have difficulty in knowing both His Will and His Mind on many critical areas of life. It is even possible to know the will of God, and yet not know His mind! Matt 6:9-10; Ephes 1:11-23; Col 1:9-13; Acts 16:6-10; Isa 3:10-11.

** the word 'Will' has several connotations. The one relevant to our Topic is, aim, design, intent, intention, and purpose. The Old and the New Testaments are described as the expressed 'will' of God.

** the word 'Mind' refers to the will (ideas, intentions or desires) that also includes the means, the timing and place of getting the will carried out.

** the mind gives/shows more details on the will.

** In many cases the date, person or place, etc, needed for the fulfilment of a particular Will of God are not mentioned.

** For discussion:

- What do we understand by 'The Will of God'?
- What do we understand by 'the 'Mind' of God?

** The Will of God - refers to the things God would want done within His Grand/Master plan both for individuals, families, Nations, and the entire Universe. They may or

 I AM ABRAHAM

may not be done if some conditions are not fulfilled.

** Mention some of the will of God that have not come to pass (and why).

On the other hand, in addition to knowing or revealing His Will, God can make His mind very clear, or clearer.

** In short, we can describe the mind of God as a clear knowledge of when, where, and through whom He wants His will done. The 'how' is still within His Sovereignty - He can decide to keep or to reveal it (perhaps, so that men will not preempt it)! E.g, Joseph, Job 5:12-14 (NLT), God still guides His own. There are four categories if God's will. There are:

* God's goodwill
* God's acceptable will
* God's perfect will, and
* God's permissive will

2.   God still Guides His own: God still guides His own. There are four categories of God's will. To know His will, some things are involved: Prayers, studying the Scriptures, and total obedience. On the other hand, to know God's mind, there are additional things to do. These include waiting upon Him in fasting, being alone with Him, and being very attentive. Psalm 25:9, 14; Rom 12:1-2; Num 22:1-20; Matt 2: 1-end; Isa 40: 28-31; I Kings 17:1-10; I Kings 18:1, 36-39; II Kings 2-3.

Conclusion: Don't gamble with life, ask God to continually fill us with the knowledge of His perfect will., and also help us to obey Him totally.

UNDERSTANDING GOD - PART VII
THE PRESENCE OF GOD (1&2)

Text: Gen 39:1-9

Introduction: By God's grace, in this study, we shall be looking at another aspect of God that is very crucial for us to understand - "The PRESENCE of God". May we desire, acquire, and never loose God's presence, in Jesus name.

Outlines:

- The Presence of God

- Manifestations of His Presence

- That they might be with Him

The Presence of God: God's presence is a reality. It is beyond a feeling (though it may or not be felt). It is also beyond an impression (even though one can have it). We can experience His Presence; we can see the manifestations of His presence. Over the ages, God had continued to reveal Himself - through His works, Acts, and ultimately through His only Begotten Son - our Lord Jesus. Col 1:11-21.

** The word 'Presence' defined:

- the state of being present

- the proximity

- an invisible spiritual being felt to be nearby

** Manifestations or Mediums of His Presence -

Mediums of His Presence - God is Sovereign: He can put His Presence in anything - wind, water, cloth, voice, words, or hands of His chosen servants; in a House, a Church Hall, etc. Among many ways, He has used the pillar of Cloud and light; Rock; Thunders, Natural disasters; The Ark; The Holy Spirit; signs and miracles, and wonders. Most importantly, He puts His Presence in His Word - He goes with His Word. Anywhere His Word goes, He is there in person. Rom 1:18-24; Isa 55:10-11; Jer 1:11-12

*** The power of His Presence: what does His Presence mean, What can the Presence of God do? - it makes all the difference!:

- between failure and success, stagnation and progress, fruitfulness and barrenness, labour and favour, Heaven and Hell, being the head or remaining as the tail, being obscure and being a monumental person. Hence the song: 'Your Presence is Heaven to me"!

- His presence also gives life, peace, satisfaction, hope, joy. For example, Joseph (Gen 39:2-5);

** (Moses - "if Your Presence will not go with us..."; Elisha - "they that be with us... II Kings 6:16; Jesus - to the Disciples: "depart not until you have been endured with power from on high"). Bro Gbile - "BABA is here".

- God's presence is everything and a lack of it is no living. Worse still, the loss of God's presence is a loss of all!

*David (Gen 16:13; I Sam 17:46-57)

*Jesus (Acts 10:38),

*Peter (Acts 2:1-48)

Attracting and Retaining His Presence - what to do:

* praise and worship

* Holy living (Gen 39:2-5; Heb 1:9)

* enlist in His Army (Mark 3:13-15; Acts 1:8);

* touch not His glory (Isa 42:8);

** Watch: when you are tempted to sin any sin, or someone is trying to provoke you to be angry - someone is behind it - his name is Satan! (John 10:10). What is he after, and what is he out to steal, to kill and to destroy? - 2 basic things:

* God's presence (ask Joseph, Samson, David, and Elisha, etc)

* Your destiny (ask Joseph, Samson, Judas, Ananias and wife)

** **Critical Prayer:** Father, please don't let anything/anyone (big or small) take Your Presence from me. Also, please let no-thing/no one (big or small) take me from Your Presence (Rom 8:35-39).

RELEASED INTO YOUR DESTINY

General Introduction

We will begin this section with the issue of direction. May the Holy Spirit teach us, in Jesus' name. Amen.

RELEASED INTO YOUR DESTINY I: DIVINE DIRECTION

Text: Psalm 32:8-11

Outline:

1. All Men Need Divine Direction

2. God Still Speaks Today

All Men Need Divine Direction

The issue of direction has to do with three things:

- Knowing where to go.

- Knowing how to get there, and

- Knowing what to do there.

These three will rarely come to us all at a go, or even so clearly at the beginning.

Also, the direction and guidance we need along the way will come forth as we obey the earlier instructions of God (Isaiah 1:19-20; 3:10-11).

The story of Joseph in Genesis 37:5-9 illustrates this. Through two different dreams, God gave him a glimpse of a very great future - God showed him that people (including his senior brothers) were bowing down to him, as well as the sun and the moon (the god, the king and leaders of Egypt). However, God did not tell him when, where, and how these would happen. As he obeyed God, running from sin, God was taking him nearer his destiny of greatness. Eventually, he got there. As we obey God step by step, we too will fulfill our destiny in Jesus' name.

It was the same with Prophet Samuel (in 1 Samuel 16:1-13). One morning, God told him: *"Stop mourning for Saul, since I have rejected him as king, take the oil, go to Jesse's house, for there, I have provided for myself a king among his sons... When you get there, I will tell you what you will do!"* Until David showed up, God did not reveal the king to-be.

 I Am Abraham

God Still Speaks Today

In one form or the other, all men need divine direction. The critical issue is, how do we get the right direction? We will look at where to go and what to do:

- Go to God - The One who is the All-knowing

    (Revelation 1:8; 3:7 John 1:5; 8:12; 14:6). Where can we find God? In His Word.

- Align our lives with His Word (Hebrews 1:9, Romans 12:1-2, Psalm 1:1-3).

- Accept His Lordship (not just His saving grace) - Yield your life totally to Him (Isaiah 1:19, John 14:15). That is, accept His will, His way, His purpose, and His timing.

- Specifically, ask Him for direction when you require it. (Psalm 32:8, Jeremiah 33:3, Daniel 2:16-23).

Note: God speaks and gives direction through many mediums. The greatest and most assuring is His WORD - the Holy Bible. So, if you want clear and divine direction, become a diligent student of the Bible (Psalm 119:18, 63, 105, 130, John 6:63, Isaiah 40:8).

- Listen and be sensitive to the Holy Spirit (John 16:13-14, 1 Corinthians 2:9-11).

- Watch out for the people who may want to play God in your life - They will suggest things that could sound good but may not necessarily be the perfect will of God! (II Kings 13:12-26).

- Not unconnected with this is the need to watch out also for people with strong, manipulating spirits, as well as schemers who have their hidden agenda (Psalm 1:1-3, 1 Corinthians 15:33).

May the Lord give us divine direction each new day in Jesus Name. May He also give us the grace to obey as He leads us.

RELEASED INTO YOUR DESTINY: PART II - DIVINE ENCOUNTER

Text: Matthew 12:22

Introduction: In part I of our study, we saw the importance of divine direction, as well as the fact that God still speaks to direct His children. We concluded the study by listing the things we must do if we will be divinely directed by God. As we continue our study, may the Holy Spirit teach us and release us to our destinies in Jesus' name. Amen.

Outline:

1. Are You Grateful?

2. Just one Encounter!

Are You Grateful?

The man in our text was possessed, blind, and dumb. Are you grateful that: you are free and not devil possessed?

That you can see, speak, hear? That you can move around by yourself?

Some questions about the man:

- Who brought him to Jesus. Is it his parents, relations, or friends, a Good Samaritan, etc.?

- Where had he gone or been taken to before - all in search of healing/deliverance? Had his problem been compounded or gotten worse? (Mark 5:25-26)

- When a person is demon or devil-possessed what is he likely to look like, or what things will he do?

- When a person is blind physically, what will he appear like, or the things he could do and not be able to do? What are the implications of being blind spiritually?

- When a person is dumb physically, what does he to look like, or things he will do or not be able to do? Even though he could appear normal, but there are somethings he could do and things he would not be able to do. What are the implications of being dumb spiritually?

- Now, when a person has all the three problems (the man here has), what will his situation/life be like?

Once again, will you be grateful to God for His mercies?

Just One Encounter!

Matt 12:22b: *"And Jesus healed him, insomuch that the blind and dumb both spake and saw"* The man entered his year of release! He was released into his destiny. All his limitations, dependency, mockery, and having to be at the mercy of people ended. (See also, Luke 5:1-9; 19:1-10, John 5:1-9; 9:1-11, Acts 3:1-9). No one encounters Jesus and remains the same again.

The greatest miracle that encountering Jesus brings is that of forgiveness for a person's sin and its guilt. Have you encountered Jesus? If not, what are you waiting for? Call upon Him where you are and just as you are! He will save you (Rom. 10:9-13; Isaiah 55:6-7; Prov. 28:13; 1 Jn. 1: 5-9).

RELEASED INTO YOUR DESTINY: PART III - DIVINE PLACEMENT

Text: Psalm 1:1-3

Introduction: In our previous study, we saw people who encountered Jesus and were released into their destiny, even as they simply obeyed what He told them (Isaiah 1:19). As we continue the series, may the Holy Spirit speak to us, in Jesus' name. Amen.

Outline:

1. Redemptive Package

2. Divine Placement

Redemptive Package

You are not an accident of nature. God has divinely packaged your life. Included in that package are His purpose (Jeremiah 1:4-5; 29:11-13), His plans, His gifts, His timing, His placements, and His blessings (among many other things).

To enable you fulfill the purpose He has for you, God has endowed you with certain gifts. He will also bring some opportunities your way. If we will fulfill God's purpose and plan for our lives, then we must learn to be where He wants us to be, and be doing what He asked us to do.

Divine Placement

It is very important to be where God wants you to be, and also be doing what He expected of you. This is what will ensure His presence and resources (John 8:29, Psalm 1:1-3, Gen 37:5-11, 12, 18, 21; 39:1-5; 41:14-16, 25, 32, 37-40). The good thing is that if you are where God asked you to be, and you are doing what He has asked you to do, even if there are challenges, God will come to your assistance (Genesis 39:7-20, 21-23; 45:1-8; 50:19-21, Isaiah 43:18-19).

Are you where God wants you to be? Are you doing God's will where He has placed you?

Prayers:

- Father, thank You for creating me in Your image and likeness. Thank You for reassuring me that I am not an accident of nature. Thank You for Your thoughts towards me.

- Thank You for Your divine package and purpose for my life. Thank You for the gifts I have discovered, and I am already using for Your glory. Thank You for the ones I am yet to discover. Please help me to maximize my life for Your glory.

- Father, help me to always know and be where You want me to be.

- I need Your presence 24/7, Father don't let me go where Your presence will not go with me.

- Father, any challenge I may be facing now where You have put me, please turn them to testimonies (Romans 8:28).

- Father, if for any reason I am not where I ought to be, please relocate me!

RELEASED INTO YOUR DESTINY: PART IV - DIVINE PRESENCE

Text: Genesis 28:10-22

Introduction: We have discussed the fact that God has a divine package for our lives. He also has a location where He must fulfill His agenda. From the story of Joseph, we saw that God can use anything and anyone to get us to our destiny. As we continue now, may the Holy Spirit teach us, in Jesus' name.

Outline:

1. Divine Presence

2. Trust and Obey

Divine Presence

God can be present in a place (Genesis 28:10-16). He can also be present with a person (Genesis 39:1-5, 21-23). The abiding presence of God is very essential. It can make the difference between success and failure, as well as between life and death (Exodus 33:15-16, 1 Samuel 16:13, 14, 18). Not only does God wants to be present with all His people, He also wants us to be carriers of His very presence (Psalm 105:14-15) However, there are conditions to fulfill.

Trust and Obey

To access and also abide in God's presence, among others, we must be holy (Psalm 15:1-5; 24:3-4, Hebrews 1:9). We must also fear Him (Proverbs 16:6, Genesis 39:7-9). Our obedience must be complete and total (Isaiah 1:19, John 8:29-30; 14:21-23). We must cultivate a life of intense praise and worship (Psalm 1:1-3; 2 Chronicles 6:11-14, Psalm 22:3). When His presence is with you, and you carry His presence, you will become unstoppable (Acts 12:5-12), you will become a channel of blessing, and an agent of transformation (Acts 1:8; 8:5-8; 10:38).

Did you once enjoy God's presence but you have lost it? You can have it back, provided you are willing to return to Him with all your heart (Proverbs 28:13). From today, and for the rest of our lives, may we experience His divine presence.

Prayer:

- Father, anything I will do that will take Your presence from me, don't let me do it.

- Father, please incapacitate anyone who is out to take me from Your presence, or take Your presence from me.

- Father, anywhere you will not go with me, don't let me ever go there.

- Father, I don't want to fail, please always be with me.

Released Into Your Destiny: Part V - Divine Security

Text: Psalm 91:1, John 10:10

Introduction: Every creature values security, particularly we human beings. In order to be secure or secure themselves, man can do anything! Security has dimensions: physical, spiritual, material, economic, career, political, etc.

Outline:

1. Why Do We Need Security

2. The Source of True Security

Why Do We Need Security?

"The thief cometh not but for to steal, to kill, and to destroy. But I have come that they might have life and have it more abundantly". (John 10:10 KJV)

There is someone called a Thief. He is one both by nature, and by his intent and acts. This thief is on an assignment, and he is already coming forth. He is on a deliberate assignment to steal, to kill, and to destroy! WATCH OUT and don't be a victim of this robber (the father of thieves and robbers).

Note: There is a difference between a thief and a robber. What do you think makes them different?

What is the thief here, out to steal? What is he out to kill? What is he out to destroy? What and Who can secure you as a person? Is it your parents, friends, spouses, government, Satan and his agents, money, position or power?

The Source of True Security

God is the source of true security! Love yourself and stay within and under His covering! There are innumerable dangers out there.

Your duty (What you must do):

- Be at alert (1 Peter 5:7-9)

- Guard your goods - Your heart, your salvation, your destiny, your relationship with God.

Good News: There is someone far greater than the Thief;

His name is JESUS. HE has come or gone ahead of the thief. Jesus said in John 10:10 that *"The thief cometh..."* meaning that he is on his way. *"But I have come..."* connotes that He is already here - far ahead of the thief. Hallelujah!

Has Jesus come ahead of the thief into your heart? If not, then there is trouble because the thief will be on a rampage and nothing can restrain him. You can still bring Jesus in, even right now (Psalm 91:1, Matthew 11:28-30).

Have you suffered some avoidable losses – all because you were not willing to bring in Jesus in earlier? I have a good news for you. If you invite Jesus in now, He can assist you to recover all that you had lost – your health, your wealth, your destiny, etc. (Please see II Cor 5:17; Isa 49:24-26; Isa 43:18-19).

RELEASED INTO YOUR DESTINY: PART VI - DIVINE PROVISION

Text: Genesis 22:12-18

Introduction: As part of His divine package for everyone He has made, God makes provisions for all they will ever need to fulfill their destiny. Unfortunately, many pass-through this world without recognizing, developing, and maximally utilizing these provisions. As we continue our series, may God open our eyes to discover, and begin to enjoy all He has given us. May we, thereby, be released into our destinies in Jesus' name.

Outline:

1. God Is the Provider

2. To Whom Much Is Given

God Is the Provider

The word provision is a compound word - Pro+vision

Pro means to be in favor or support of something, or to enhance it.

Vision means the ability to see; something that you imagine - a picture that you see in your mind; something you dream about or you see in your dream.

God is the Provider. He has a vision and a mission in mind when He made you and me. That vision or mission is called Purpose - the reason why He made us (Jeremiah 1:4-5).

There are many things God has made available to support, enhance, and help us fulfill our destinies. As the Creator and Maker/Enabler, God Himself is our number one provision and provider. God's provisions are both physical, spiritual, material, financial, emotional, etc. Who and what are the other provisions/helpers? They include our parents (especially mothers), spouses, brothers (both biological and spiritual), friends, and even enemies. They also include our gifts, events, appointments (and disappointments), etc. (Proverbs 18:16, Genesis 37-41; 45:1-8, 1 Samuel 17:1-end, Luke 5:1-7).

Gifts can broadly be categorized into three: innate gifts (or natural abilities and talents), acquired skills and competencies, as well as spiritual gifts. The stories of Joseph (Genesis 37-50) and David (1 Samuel 16:14-22, 18) shed light on these. God, in His Sovereignty, uses all things for His purposes in our lives (Romans 8:28).

To Whom Much Is Given (Luke 12:48)

Don't be a prodigal! Don't waste or abuse God's provisions that are meant to help you fulfill, or take you to your destiny. If you abuse or waste them, you will never be able to fulfill your God-given purpose and destiny. Even though the Bible called one young man a Prodigal Son (Luke 15:10-32), there were many other prodigal children (sons and daughters) in the Bible. They include Esau, Reuben, Ephraim, Samson, Gehazi, Solomon, Dinah, Jezebel, Judas, etc.

As a beautiful young lady, are you selling your body? If yes, then you are a prodigal! Today may you repent, and may God give you a brand-new beginning, in Jesus' name (Isaiah 43:18-19).

RELEASED INTO YOUR DESTINY: PART VII - DIVINE ENABLEMENT

Text: Psalm 124:1-8, Zechariah 4:6-9

Introduction: We thank God for all He continues to use His word to do in our lives, particularly since we began the series. As we continue, may the Lord open our eyes of understanding in Jesus' name.

Outline:

1. Creator and Enabler

2. Looking Unto Jesus

Creator and Enabler

God is not just the Creator and Maker, He is also the Enabler. He has the power to make and unmake, to enable and disable! (Genesis 1:1-3; Revelation 4:11, Psalm 127:1, John 15:5, Deuteronomy 32:39). Except He helps us, no one else can help us. Except He enables and empowers us, we can never succeed in life. In Psalm 124, King David enumerated some of the things the enemy would have done if God had not been on his side. They include unbridled attacks, burning anger, being swallowed up, being engulfed with waters, overwhelming and raging waters, tearing teeth, hunted life, etc. Thank God that He was on the side of David (and of His people - the Israelites) - Psalm 124:7-8, Romans 8:31. The God who made a way of escape for David will make a way for us, in Jesus' name.

Looking Unto Jesus

In life, there are many things we would have loved to be and do, but which we are unable to. This can be due to several factors - both physical and spiritual. For some, it may be the lack of the means, or it may not be God's perfect will. Yet for some, the enemy may be at work to hinder. This is why it becomes critical for us to (among other things):

(i)   Know the mind of God on every area of life, both in small and big things, in the short and long run (Psalm 25:9, 14)

(ii) Submit ourselves to God's perfect will (Isaiah 45:9-10, James 4:7-8, 10)

(iii) Recognize that we have an enemy whose primary assignment is to prevent us from knowing and fulfilling our destiny (1 Peter 5:7-9)

(iv) Learn to give God all the praise and glory for all He continues to do in our lives, and also believe Him for the next (Philippians 4:6-8, NLT)

(v) Do not let the so-called success of others make us think God has forgotten us (Psalm 92:7, 12-15, Hebrews 13:5-6, Romans 8:28, Jeremiah 22:13, Habakkuk 2:12).

BEHOLD, HE COMETH!

General Introduction

Someone said if you want to know what a book is all about, read the first and the last chapters! This made me decide that with God's help, in the year 2020, I would concentrate on two books of the Bible - Genesis and Revelation - the First and last books of the Bible. I didn't even know that covid-19 was coming. Thank God, the lockdown helped me greatly (Romans 8:28).

The book of Genesis tells us how and where it all began. It also tells us about all that God did, particularly as God decided to pick a man called Abram (whose name He later changed to Abraham). Through this single man, God raised a whole nation - Israel, which He, the Almighty God planned to use as a model. The entire Old Testament is the story of that nation (Israel). The New Testament is a new chapter in human history, as God Himself decided to visit and walk upon this earth (John 1:14-18).

The New Testament has 3 parts:

- The Gospels - Covering the life and ministry of Jesus, His death, resurrection, and ascension to Heaven, as well as the Great Commission.

- The Acts of the Apostles and the Epistles - Which explain the spread of the Gospel from Jerusalem to the entire Gentile world.

- The book of Revelation - Which tells in great detail when and how everything will end.

Without any doubt, we are at the end of the age. All the things prophesied or predicted in the Bible have virtually been fulfilled. The Lord Jesus – our Saviour and Bridegroom – will soon appear: *"This is all the more urgent, for you know how late it is; time is running out. Wake up, for our salvation is nearer now than when we first believed. 12 The night is almost gone; the day of salvation will soon be here. So remove your dark deeds like dirty clothes, and put on the shining armor of right living. 13 Because we belong to the day, we must live decent lives for all to see. Don't participate in the darkness of wild parties and drunkenness, or in sexual promiscuity and immoral living, or in quarreling and jealousy. 14 Instead, clothe yourself with the presence of the Lord Jesus Christ. And don't let yourself think about ways to indulge your evil desires"*. Romans 13:11-14 (NLT). May He find us ready, in Jesus' name. Amen.

BEHOLD HE COMETH! (PART I)

Text: Revelation 1:5-8

"and from Jesus Christ, the faithful witness, the firstborn from the dead, and the ruler over the kings of the earth. To Him who loved us and washed us from our sins in His own blood, and has made us kings and priests to His God and Father, to Him be glory and dominion forever and ever. Amen. Behold, He is coming with clouds, and every eye will see Him, even they who pierced Him. And all the tribes of the earth will mourn because of Him. Even so, Amen. "I am the Alpha and the Omega, the Beginning and the End," says the Lord, "who is and who was and who is to come, the Almighty."

Outlines:

1. Understanding the signs of the times

2. Surely, Jesus is coming soon

Understanding the Signs of the Times

The times we are in can be looked at from at least 3 dimensions:

* Physical (socio-political, economic, climate, etc); Technological (inventions and digitalization, etc); and, Spiritual (end-time prophecies as they affect the World, Unbelievers, and Believers).

Let us look at all these in some more details.

In the physical realm, today, some men continue to live, act, and even claim that there is no God, and that Man is not accountable to any superior Being that could be described as God! They claim that they are in charge here (on earth). They are gods, and must define what is right and wrong, and what is the truth or untruth. Hence, like the Biblical Sodom and Gomorrah or the Prodigal Son, our societies are filled with all kinds of sexualising perversions, riotous living, violence, injustice, wickedness, etc. The consequences? Unlimited chaos and confusion!

In the area of Technology, discoveries, breakthroughs and innovations continue to occur. From basic devices to complicated ones. High Towers and Skyscrapers continue to compete in heights across our capital cities. The same goes for communications, and digital revolution – cloning, robotic engineering, (Artificial Intelligence), electronic man, etc, are now common words in our vocabularies. Of course, there are pros and cons to all these.

The Spiritual realm, though seemingly unclear to many, is the actual realm where the most significant events are going on. In truth, all we are seeing in the physical and Technological domains are mere shadows or glimpses of the spiritual realm. Issues like New World Order, Globalisation or *"One Everything"* – One World Government, One World Economic Order, One World Religion. Global, Jihad, Apostasy, and the unbridled resistance to the Gospel, etc, are all mere manifestation. (1 Chronicle 12:32, Matthew 16:1-4; 1 Timothy 4:1-3; 2 Timothy 3:1-9.)

All the three realms (physical, technological, and spiritual), affect each other, and also affect all who dwell here on the earth. In our age of digital revolution and information explosion, there is no information you need on anything that you cannot find on the internet. All you need is to just Google it!

In spite of her great knowledge, discoveries, devices, and socio-political breakthroughs, we find that the world has a great limitation, it is ignorant of things that matter mist!

"Behold what manner of love the Father has bestowed on us, that we should be called children of God! Therefore the world does not

knowus, because it did not know Him." 1 John 3:1

The decision-makers of the world are ignorant of the most crucial thing. The world does not know us (true Believers), because it did not know Him (our great God)! The world is ignorant of the very thing that matters most - the knowledge of God - His character, principles, power, purpose, and plans (Acts 10:34-35). They also forget that God is to be feared. From Adam down the line - Noah's generation, Tower of Babel, Moses, Samson, Eli, David, Solomon, Gehazi; Ananias and wife, etc.

In Romans 8:32, the Bible said God did not even spare His own Son. If He did not spare Him, He won't spare or exonerate the world that has ignored Him and flagrantly broken His laws!

What is the sum of all these? Men had been having their own ways. Now, it's God's time to begin to have His way! (Revelation 11:12-18, Genesis 19:14-17)

Surely, Jesus is coming soon! At His first coming, He came as a Lamb. This time, He is coming as the Bridegroom, as the Lion, as the Judge, the Rewarder, and the King of Kings. (John 14:1-3, Acts 1:6-11, Hebrews 10:37-38, 1 Thessalonians 4:13-18, Revelation 1:7-8; 5:5, 6:10; 19:16, 22:10-12, Matthew 5:12; 25:1-13, 31, 1 Peter 4:5, Colossians 3:24, 1 Timothy 6:15).

Conclusion: In a time like this, don't be ignorant. Rather, be alive unto righteousness, seek to know God the more. Seek to know His agenda or calendar. Don't let Christ's return meet you like a thief in the night - unaware and unprepared

Prayers:

- Father, thank You for Your truth that sets free.

- Father, deliver me from ignorance of things that matter. Help me to seek the right knowledge.

- Father, don't let me miss the Rapture.

BEHOLD HE COMETH! (PART II)

Text: Matthew 24:1-44

Introduction: In Part I of this series, we emphasized the need to be conversant with the signs of the times we are in. We also invited our attention to the fact that Jesus is surely coming back. As we continue the series, our focus here is on the signs that will help us to know how close or imminent the coming of our Lord is. We shall also look at the manner of His coming. May the Holy Spirit open our understanding in Jesus' name. Amen.

Outlines:

1. The Signs of His Coming

2. The Manner of His Coming

 I AM ABRAHAM

The Signs of His Coming

In response to the 3-in-1 questions of His disciples, our Lord gave us some hints regarding His second coming. In all, there are 16 signs. Virtually all had come to pass in varying degrees. Hence, the need to be alert and get ready. (Matthew 24:1-44, Romans 13:11-15, 2 Peter 5:7-11, Ecclesiastes 7:8).

For Reflection: Let's look at each of the signs. How many had happened, are happening, are yet to happen? As an individual, which one do you consider so touchy and probably is/are giving you concern and challenging you to be more prepared for the Lord's return?

The Manner of His Coming

The Second coming of the Lord will be in two stages:

- The Rapture - Catching up of genuinely saved souls.

- The Revelation - The Return of Jesus to the earth.

(1 Thessalonians 4:13-18, 1 Corinthians 15:52, Matthew 16:27, Revelation 1:7-8, Acts 1:9-11, Matthew 24:30; 25:31, 2 Peter 3:1-13)

During the gap in between, two simultaneous events will be going on - one in Heaven (the Marriage Supper of the Lamb) and the other on earth (the great tribulation).

It is to be noted that while there are clear signs about Christ's physically returning to the earth, there are no signs to alert us about when the Rapture will occur. Knowing and being convinced that Jesus is coming is very crucial. However, the most crucial is being ready whenever He comes, and it could be today!

The only inference we can reasonably make from the Scriptures is that the interval between the Rapture and the Revelation (Christ's physical return to earth) is about seven years.

Conclusion: Watch and do not be deceived! Christ's coming is sure and certain (Matthew 24:10-13, 2 Peter 3:3-10). While we are to plan and work as if He will not be coming for another century, we must live a holy and pure life all the time, as if He will return today!

Prayers:

Song: When You come and collect Your people, remember me O Lord...

- Father, please help me to be ready when You come to take the Saints home to Heaven

- Everything the enemy may want to use to distract/divert my focus, don't let him succeed in my life and family.

- The grace to be more watchful and more faithful, please pour upon me today and right now.

BEHOLD HE COMETH! (PART III)

Text: 2 Peter 3:3-12

Introduction: Having so far realized the fact that Jesus is coming back soon, two issues now become very important; how to be ready, as well as how to be occupied for Him. In this study, we will concentrate on the former.

Outlines:

i) The inner man

ii) The outer man

The Inner Man

In most of His teachings and parables, our Lord always used the known to make the unknown clearer. In particular, He used the Parable of the Ten Virgins to show us who He is coming back for, and what such people need to doing order to be ready for His Coming. Apostle Paul also used the relationship between husband and wife to illustrate who we must be. In all, we are to be waiting for and expecting the coming of our Bridegroom. (Matthew 25:1-13, Ephesians 5:23-27, Ephesians 5:1-8, Hebrews 12:14, Psalm 15:1-5, Romans 12:1-2)

A look at the Ten Virgins:

They had a good/great goal/objective: They went forth to meet the Bridegroom.

Matters Arising:

- The Bridegroom tarried. Did He deliberately tarry or something on the way which He had to attend to, or do, delayed Him? (Mark 5:24-34; 10:46-52).

The truth: Mercy or compassion delayed Him.

- While the Bridegroom tarried, tiredness/weariness set in. The Virgins also began to slumber. Eventually they slept!

Verse 6 - At midnight, there was a shout, "The Bridegroom cometh, go ye out to meet Him."

Verse 7 - They all arose or woke up (i.e. from slumber and sleep). Then they trimmed their lamp.

Verse 10 - While the five (who didn't have extra oil went to buy), the Bridegroom came, only those who were ready went in with Him to the marriage, and the door was shut!

The Outer Man

Man is a tripartite being. What should we be focusing all of our being and resources upon in a time like this? (Colossians 3:1-4, Galatians 5:13-24, Ephesians 5:1-8 Psalm 1:1-3; 119:11; 119:97-104, 1 Peter 4:7-11; Matthew 6:19-21; 25-33, Hebrews 12:14, Romans 12:9-10 - NLT)

Conclusion: Let's pay attention to ourselves (in and out). Let us daily purify our hearts, and be ready for our Lord. May He help us to the end, in Jesus' name.

Prayers:

- Father, make me holy - in and out. Deliver me from things that easily pollute.

- Father, help me to maximize my life and resources for Your glory.

- Father, as I study Your Word, transform me, and help me to discover Your perfect will for my life.

- Father, in this end time, keep Your Church focused on things that matter.

BEHOLD HE COMETH! (PART IV)

Text: Luke 19: 11-27

Introduction: We have looked at who we ought to be, even as we prepare for the coming of the Lord. Now, we shall continue by looking at what we should be occupied with. May the Holy Spirit speak to us, in Jesus' name, Amen.

Outlines:

1. Occupy Till I come

2. The Kingdom Lifestyle

Occupy Till I Come

In a time like this, we are to be occupied with the Kingdom Business (and not just Church or denomination, but Kingdom Business). To do this effectively, two things are critical:

(a) We must know and preach the core messages of the Kingdom.

(b) We must live a Kingdom Lifestyle.

What it means to occupy:

- To engage the attention or energies of,

- To take up (a place or extent in space),

- To take or hold possession or control of - this world that I'm leaving you in (John 17:11-18),

- To fill or perform the functions of (an office or position),

- To reside in as an owner (or tenant),

The Core messages of the Kingdom are in two dimensions:

1. <u>To the world</u> - Earlier, it was "Repent! for the Kingdom of Heaven is at hand." Now it should be, "Repent, for the judgment of God is near!"

2. <u>To the Saints</u> - Prepare, the Lord's coming is at hand!

(John 1:22-27, Luke 3:7-16; 12:35-40; 19:5-10; 19:11-27, Acts 2:37-41; 3:11-21, Hebrews 2:1-3; 12:14, Jude 1:7, 14-16; Matthew 5:13-16; 28:18-20; 2 Peter 3:3-12, 1 Peter 1:15-16, Ephesians 5:1-8)

 I AM ABRAHAM

The Kingdom Lifestyle

In a time like this, as we show concern for the world, and get occupied in bringing them to the knowledge of Truth, we should ensure that we too are qualified for (and not left out of) the Kingdom. We are to live a Kingdom lifestyle through the following:

(i) Daily self-examination

(ii) Knowing our Enemy - Satan!

(iii) Running for our lives - fleeing and abstaining from all appearances of the devil.

(iv) Holding fast to that which we have, lest someone takes our crown

(v) Letting nothing separate us from the love of Christ

(vi) Being Kingdom-minded

(vii) Possessing the Kingdom Keys

(viii) Being our brother's keeper.

(Genesis 4:8-12, 1 Corinthians 9:24-27; 10:12-13, Matthew 5:13-16, Isaiah 60:1-3, 1 Thess. 5:22, Revelation 12:7-9, John 14:6, Romans 6:23; 8:35-39; 14:17, 1 John 1:4-10; Jude 1:3-4).

Conclusion: Essentially, every follower of Christ must live a holy life, love others, particularly the believers; be ready for the coming of the Lord, and spread the Gospel of Jesus to all the world. May we not fail in any of these, in Jesus' name.

Prayers:

- Father, help me to be occupied with things that matter in Your reckoning.

- Father, please let my life be Kingdom-oriented.

- Father, it's by Your mercy we can be qualified and ready. Please have mercy on us to the end.

- Father, don't let me be guilty of doing what I ask others not to do. Also, don't let me be guilty of not doing what I ask others to do (1 Cor. 9:27).

- Father, in my zeal to be salt the earth, as well as the light of the world, please don't let me lose my own salt and light (Matt. 5:13-16).

BEHOLD HE COMETH! (PART V)

Text: 1 Peter 1:13-25

Introduction: Jesus is coming again to do three main things: to receive His people unto Himself, to judge the world, and to reign over the earth. As we said in the conclusion of part IV of our study, every follower of Christ must live a holy life, love others (particularly the believers), be ready for the coming of the Lord, and spread the Gospel of Jesus to all the world. We shall be discussing the very important issue of Holiness. May the Holy Spirit Himself make us holy even as we expect our Lord's return, in Jesus' name. AMEN.

Outlines:

1. Be Ye Holy

2. Holiness - A Necessity

Be Ye Holy

Very often, the questions are asked: what is holiness? Why must we live holy? How can I be Holy? We should be careful not to mistake morality for holiness. There are many good, moral people all around us, but they are not necessarily holy. Morality is living within the moral law. Holiness, on the other hand, is imbibing the character of God. It is partaking of the Holy nature of God so that our thoughts, our words, our desires, motives and our actions become godly.

There are many reasons to be holy:

(i) Holiness is God's will for all His people.

(ii) We are children of a holy God. God – our Father – is holy.

(iii) He has redeemed us to be a holy bride for His Holy Son - Jesus.

(iv) We represent a holy God.

(v) We will soon meet our holy Lord. We, therefore, need to be holy because of the Lord's return. (1 Thessalonians 5:23, Leviticus 19:1-2, 1 Peter 1:15-16, Ephesians 5:25-27, 1 John 2:28; 3:2-3, 2 Corinthians 7:1, Hebrews 12:10, 2 Peter 3:10-14, Titus 2:11-14.)

 I Am Abraham

Holiness - A Necessity

There is a need to seek to be holy in all areas of our lives, especially in our thoughts, our words, our motives, our actions, and relationships. The following will surely help to make us holy:

(i)   The Word of God

(ii) The fullness of the Holy Spirit - He is the Holy Spirit, He has the power and ministry to make us holy. It is the Holy Spirit that can prepare us for the coming of the Lord. God the Father and Jesus our Saviour too have a role to play in making us holy (John 17:19).

(iii) Daily commitment to a holy living (John 14:30; 17:17, Psalm 1:1-3; 119:11, 63, Romans 12:1-2, 2 Timothy 3:16-17, Ephesians 5:18, Luke 9:23, 2 Corinthians 6:14-18, 1 Corinthians 15:33)

Conclusion: Whether it is today, or it will be much later, let us keep on preparing for the Lord's coming. Let us live each day expecting Him (2 Peter 3:10-14). May we not be left behind when He comes in Jesus' name.

Prayers:

- Father, thank You for the assurance that Jesus is coming again. Please help me to be ready.

- Father, I am determined to live holy, please help my determination.

- Father, separate me from anyone or anything that will prevent me from being ready.

- Father, fill me with Your Holy Spirit and let Him help me to always know what to do.

BEHOLD HE COMETH! (PART VI) AT EASE IN ZION?

Text: Amos 6:1-8

Introduction: So far, we concentrated most of our discussions on ourselves - we who by God's grace have known the Lord, as well as what we need to do to be qualified to go with our Lord when He returns soon. We will agree that there are multitudes both within and out of the Church who are ignorant of happenings in these end times. We owe it a duty to tell them. May the Lord Himself open our eyes of understanding in Jesus' name. Amen.

Outline:

1. The Bliss of Ignorance

2. Sound the Alarm in Zion!

The Bliss of Ignorance

There are many Christians who are ignorant of, or are deceived about the true nature of God, as well as His endtime agenda for the world. This could partly be because they are lost sheep under lost shepherds! There is also an uncountable number of unbelievers who live their daily lives oblivious of the imminent return of Jesus, the King of Kings. We are to pray and do all we can to reach them. (Hosea 4:6, John 8:32, 36; 14:1-3, 6, Acts 4:11-12, Luke 17:2030, Zechariah 11:15-17, Jonah 1:1-3; 3:5-10, Romans 1:16-18, 19-28)

The word "Bliss" means complete happiness. The opposite of it is calamity, misery, sadness, wretchedness! The ungodly lives that people live will surely earn them infinite calamity and trouble after death! In the tract, "Genuine Peace", the writer talked about true or genuine peace, and a peace that is displayed out of ignorance of what is at stake.

"My people are destroyed for lack of knowledge. Because you have rejected knowledge, I also will reject you from being priest for Me; Because you have forgotten the law of your God, I also will forget your children." Hosea 4:6

Sound the Alarm in Zion!

As God's children who, by His grace, are conversant with

 I AM ABRAHAM

God's end-time agenda, we must sound the alarm - to wake up the sleeping and slumbering Christians as well as the ignorant and deceived ones. We are also to do all we can, and use all we have to reach the unbelievers. (Joel 2:1-3, Ephesians 5:14, Romans 13:11-14, 2 Peter 3:7-12, 2 Corinthians 5:18-21, Revelation 6:1-17; 13:9-14, Isaiah 55:67)

There are some things I read in the Bible that make me afraid about God. For example, His judgments that are with no respect for persons! (Deut. 27:12-23; 1 Kings 11:1-11; Acts 10:34-35). In addition to personal (physical) witnessing/preaching, we are to use all social media platforms to reach more people with the Good News – Gospel (Rom.1:16).

Conclusion: While we go after souls to get them to the Kingdom, we are to keep on watching over our own lives. May we, too, never be disqualified in Jesus' name.

(Matthew 5:13-16, 1 Corinthians 9:27).

 **APPENDIX**

PROGRAMMING FOR SUCCESS

A - Here, we will begin with some productivity enhancement hints:

(i) Personal Growth - Begin each day with The Owner of your life and the new day. Acquaint yourself with "THE FIRST VOICE"

(ii) Family (Spouse and Children)

As much as possible, try to attend one or two marriage enrichment seminars in a year

(iii) Work/Ministry - Pay attention to your main assignments, as well as your leader. Improve your leadership through reading and self-development, too.

The Assignment:

- Know the key, critical and core elements and things to attend to.

- Pray and study the Word to get inspiration and direction. Then pray more for clarity and direction and timing (knowing the will and the mind of God)

- Your Leader:

  - Know his or her passion/drive

  - Know the performance questions that he or she will ask you (spiritual, numerical and financial growth issues).

Your own Leadership Development:

- Pursue knowledge - Commit yourself to learning and reading! Ask yourself, and answer the question: Which/what book am I currently reading?

As much as possible, have weekly schedules:

- Monday – Learning, Reading, Knowledge, Writing, etc

- Tuesday and Thursday - Work/Ministry (admin and strategies)

- Wednesday - Family – (from noon downwards).

- Friday to Sunday - programmes/ministrations, etc.

(iii) Writing of books:

Why write books - "To influence people I will never meet - books increase my audience and my message" - Les Parrott.

- To have global influence for God - Reach those I may not be able to reach by direct or face to face contacts.

Note where your friends, your history were. But also, where your future lies. Your future may not necessarily be where your friends and history are! Then move on! So you can chart a new territory, leave all you know and learn what you did not know (Gen. 12:1-5).

B - Making Each Day Count

Note that each day is an unrepeatable miracle. Today will never happen again, hence the need to make it count! Make it your masterpiece. Have core areas for focus every day:

Faith: Bring God into the picture every day. Look at everything with God in the picture, it will give you a sense of security and resilience (Rom. 8:28; Psalm 1:1-3).

In a practical sense,

- Begin and end your day with God (Psalm 92:1-2)
- First Voice: Hear God's Voice first every day! Let God's Voice/Word shape your heart, your day, your life, and your destiny. God's Voice/Word sanctifies, gives light, direction, inspires (Jn. 17:17; Rom. 12:1-2; Psalm 119:105,130).

- Before going to bed at night, look back and give Him all the glory and praise. (Psalm 92:2)

  - **Family:** My definition of success is having those who are closest to me love and respect me the most. Why? Because if those who really know me don't respect me, it means I'm not living right and doing what I should!

  - **Relationship:** Success is a relationship game. Take time and trouble to understand people and build relationships, the dividends will be very great.

Note: The most sought-after skill is the ability to communicate. Those who can will always be in demand.

  - **Mission:** What is my mission and goal in life? It is to add value, that is make something (people, place, system, the world, etc.) far better than I met it. The question is, am I actually doing that? Give your personal attention to your mission every day, and you will never stray away from it, someday in the future.

  - **Health:** You need discipline to take care of your health daily! Eating right, and exercising daily are things that are easy to neglect! Work on your health daily.

  - **C - Being Conformed to the Image of Christ**

Note the following about Christ:

- Christ knew the Heart of God.

- He knew the purposes of God.

- He knew the ways of God.

- He ordered His life so the Father could accomplish His purposes through Him.

Prayer:

- Father, please teach/reveal to me Your heart, Your purposes, and Your ways.

- Father, please help me to order my life aright so You can accomplish Your purposes through me.

- Father, please show me and teach me what to do and how to do it. Also, please give me the grace and wisdom to do it timely.

New Order:

- Right priorities - lifestyle, time management - in the Word (First Voice, worship, prayers, etc.).

- The RULE of 5: Every day read, write, think, ask questions, and file what you learn!

 NOTES

1. Autobiography – IDOWU, Moses Oludele: "David Olulana Babajide ' The Last of The Mighty Ones, the Untold Story of One of Africa's Notable Prophets of the 20th Century" – Divine Artillery Publications, 2012.

2. AKANNI, Gbile "He Leads Me – (My Personal Stories From The Days of My Youth" – Peace House Publishing Team, 2021.

3. "WELCOME TO PATMOS" – pp129 - A large part of this Chapter was first used by the author in "THE FIRST VOICE – Sunrise Foundation International, Australia, 2017.

4. Spiritual Reading – Pp 168.

5. Proverbs 18:16 – *"A man's gift makes room for him, And brings him before great men."*

6. Matt 11:12 – *"And from the days of John the Baptist until now the kingdom of heaven suffers violence, and the violent take it by force."*

7. Matt 19:12 – *"For there are eunuchs who were born thus from their mother's womb, and there are eunuchs who were made eunuchs by men, and there are eunuchs who have made themselves eunuchs for the kingdom of heaven's sake. He who is able to accept it, let him accept it." Jesus Blesses Little Children*

8. "State Pastors" – is a leadership level in the hierarchical set up of the RCCG. At this level, the pastor oversees several parishes or assemblies.

ACKNOWLEDGMENTS

Living for seventy years had been by God's special grace. Part of that grace is that God had brought multitudes of people to be a blessing to me - beginning with the very womb where I was formed (Psalm 139:13-16). All these people are my Destiny Helpers.

More than forty-one of my seventy years of life I have now spent in the The Redeemed Christian Church of God (RCCG). I owe what I am today to the grace of God (I Cor 15:9-10). This amazing grace and the favours it continued to attract to me came from three sources which I cannot afford be silent about but rather must profusely acknowledge. First, is to the friend who introduced me to the RCCG- Bro (now Pastor) Bayo Adeyokunnu. Next are my spiritual parents – Daddy Enoch Adejare, and Mummy Folu ADEBOYE (General Overseer & Mother-In-Israel of RCCG). The love, interest, and confidence they developed and reposed in me over these many years can only be God-breathed. All these are in spite of all that many self-seeking blackmailers, and destiny derailers had said, and done

ACKNOWLEDGMENTS

(Psalm 89:1, 22-24). May the Almighty God uphold you both to the very end, and also help you to finish your races well – without scandal, without scar, and without shame in the Mighty Name of Jesus.

In getting this autobiography done, many people came to my mind. I can group them into three: family; workplace and ministry; and friends.

Firstly, I thank all my senior brothers. Two of them, in particular, funded my education from Secondary School up to University. It must have been a huge sacrifice!

In the workplace and in ministry, the list is endless - both locally and on foreign missions. I thank members of the Lagos State Secretariat Fellowship, Alausa-Ikeja, members of the various RCCG House Fellowships in Ikoyi and Victoria Islands of Lagos, as well as the churches that grew therefrom. I cannot forget Pastors Adegboye and Oretayo Adetola; Peter and Theresa Chanda of Lusaka, Zambia; Brethren in Guam, Saipan, New Zealand, several Pacific Island nations including Solomon Islands, Fiji, PNG, Vanuatu, and Samoa etc.

I specially thank elderly friends and leaders including Elders Felix Ohiwerei, Fola Aboaba, Simeon Olakunri, Joseph Obayemi, Kayode Oshundahunsi, Rev John Dansu, Pastor Peter Adeyemi (Daddy Mate). Friends and Colleagues including Okey Mofunanya, Dipo Kalejaiye, Pastors Remi Oluboba, Sanya Kolajo, Francis Oluwalade, Joshua

Owojuyigbe, Stephen Jagun, Abiodun Doherty, Drs. Olaitan Oyefeso, John Adegboye, Isaac Adewumi, Femi and Faith Odumade, Kunle Oresegun, Niyi Borire, Vincent Adegborioye, just to mention a few.

A great editing work went into the final preparation of this book. I thank Pastor Sam Olaniyan for the valuable time he devoted to joining me in doing this. Also, I thank Enoch Alimi for the cover design.

Finally, on immediate family front, I thank Jane Adesola – my wife of over thirty-six years – for all her love, prayers, diligence, patience, and endurance. May the Lord Himself reward you abundantly, in Jesus' name. To Tolulope and Temitope – the two wonderful children who God gave us, may the God of Abraham multiply and make you into Nations (Gen 17:16).

Abraham Haastrup, Melbourne, Australia.
June, 2022.

AUTHOR'S PROFILE

Background

Abraham Haastrup hails from the Royal Ajimoko Haastrup family of Ilesha, Osun State of Nigeria. He was born on the 11th of January, 1952 to David Adebiyi and Florence Tinuola Abebi Haastrup.

He attended the Apostolic Primary Schools Oke Ooye, and Igbogi/Ikoyi – Ilesha; Atakumosa High School, Osu-Ilesha; the Ibadan Polytechnic; the University of Ibadan.

On graduation from the University of Ibadan in June 1980, Abraham Adewole went for his one year mandatory National Youth Service Corps (NYSC) in Ondo State and was posted to Awo-Ekiti Grammar School. He, thereafter, taught briefly at St Joseph Boys' High School, Atunrase, Surulere, Lagos before joining the Lagos State Internal Revenue Board as a Tax Administrator in April 1982. He moved into the Lagos State Administrative Cadre in January 1983.

In 1986, Abraham Adewole attended the Post-Graduate Diploma course in Public Administration at the University of Ife (now OAU). In 1989, he was granted the British Council Technical Assistance Scholarship to study at the University of Birmingham, England where he obtained a Masters of Social Science in Development Finance.

Abraham Adewole returned to Nigeria in 1990 and in answer to God's call upon his life, finally voluntarily withdrew his service from the Lagos State Government on the 31st of March 1992.

Spiritual life and Ministry

Abraham Adewole had earlier joined the Redeemed Christian Church of God (RCCG) as an ordinary member in August 1981 shortly after his conversion. He became a worker, was ordained as an Assistant Pastor in 1988, and a Full Pastor in August 1993.

Having been specifically called by God (in May 1990) into International Missions, Abraham returned to Nigeria from Britain in November of the same year to start preparing for Full-time Ministry.

On the 1st of April 1992, along with his wife, Jane Adesola, he resumed as a full-time Minister in the RCCG. He was initially posted to RCCG VI/Ikoyi family to work under the leadership of Pastor Adegboye Adetola of blessed memory.

He was sent to Zambia immediately after the 1993 August Convention of the RCCG, as a pioneer missionary. He became Area and Zonal Pastor respectively in 1994 and 1996.

Appointments

At the August 1997 Convention, He was appointed as State Pastor for Osun, and transferred to Osogbo. In September 2001, he was promoted as the State Coordinator for Ondo and Ekiti States, and transferred to Akure. Following a new and major leadership restructuring in the RCCG (that saw the emergence of the "Special Assistants" Cadre, Abraham was appointed (along with nine others) as a Special Assistant to the General Overseer (SATGO) and Regional Pastor, and transferred to Lagos. As a SATGO, he was asked to be in charge of Admin and Personnel - a portfolio he shared with Pastor Olu Obanure (of blessed memory). As a Regional Pastor, He was in charge of Lagos Region 2 made up of ten (10) Provinces, with Headquarters based in Somolu, Lagos.

Current Appointments

In August 2010, following another major leadership reorganization, he was transferred to Australia as SATGO and Regional Pastor for RCCG Oceania (made up of Australia and about 28 Pacific Island nations). In August 2018, he was promoted as an Assistant General Overseer for RCCG Australia and South Pacific Regions.

Finally, following a recent global restructuring of the RCCG operations, on January 11th 2021, Pastor Haastrup was appointed the Continental Overseer in charge of Australia/Pacific Continent of the RCCG - the position he occupies till date. To God be all the glory!

Other Ministerial Engagements

In addition to all his regular appointments, Abraham at various times was a member and Secretary of the RCCG Salary Review Committee (set up to attend to welfare of the entire RCCG Staff), under the able leaderships of Daddy DA Ilori, and later Daddy Tunji Onileaja. In 2008, he was appointed Chairman of the SRC. Also, Haastrup served as Assistant Secretary, Secretary, and later Chairman of the RCCG World Advisory Committee (WAC) - a body set up by the General Overseer to constantly and strategically view and review the operational modalities of the RCCG as an organization.

The call into missions made Abraham to take special interests in reading about international missions. It also motivated him to keenly follow RCCG mission policies, activities, as well as challenges, even as the Lord opens doors to take the Church to the nations.

To enhance his ministry calling, Abraham Adewole obtained M.A in Christian Leadership from the West African Theological Seminary (WATS) Lagos, Nigeria. He is also an Alumnus of the Haggai Institute, Singapore; International Institute of Leadership (ILI, USA), etc.

Presently, he and his wife, Jane Adesola, are serving God as missionaries in Australia/Pacific Continent of the RCCG. Christian mission work has taken Wole Haastrup to Britain, Germany, East Africa, USSR, etc. He has also travelled across the length and breadth of Australia and several South Pacific Islands.

Abraham Adewole's marriage is blessed with two adult children – Tolulope and Temitope.

Publications

Abraham Adewole has been enabled by God to write some books. These include:

1. God Still Speaks Today (Almond Tree Books, Lagos)

2. High Praise (Almond Tree Books, Lagos 1995)

3. Obedience - The Secret of Miracles (Almond Tree Books, Lagos 1995)

4. In Remembrance of Me (Almond Tree Books, Lagos 2001)

5. Your Last Hope (Almond Tree Books, Lagos 2003)

6. The Secret of Divine Favour (Almond Tree Books, Lagos 2003)

7. The Christian Worker (Sunrise Foundation International, Melbourne, 2014)

8. Ebenezer (God Can Do it Again) – (Sunrise Foundation International, Melbourne, 2014)

9. The Almighty Formulae (Sunrise Foundation International, Melbourne, 2015)

10. Nations at Rage (Sunrise Foundation International, Melbourne, 2015)

11. The FIRST VOICE (Sunrise Foundation International, Melbourne, 2017)

12. Overcoming Giants (Global Kingdom Influence, 2022)

13. The Third Epistles (A Leadership Reminiscence) - Global Kingdom Influence, 2021).

To God be the glory!

www.ingramcontent.com/pod-product-compliance
Lightning Source LLC
Chambersburg PA
CBHW050304010526
44107CB00055B/2097